On The Virge
The Journey of a Lifetime

To Jodi, Lynn, Joe, Brian, Makenna, Keegan and Nora, and hopefully others to come. My prayer is that one day you may pick up this book and remember that God is your ultimate travel companion on this Journey we call Life.

To Shaunda. You are the greatest friend I have ever had. Watching you on this Journey has been one of the greatest adventures of my life. Thanks for dreaming with me.

And Matt, you are not forgotten. Your ministry is not yet complete. You still touch lives today from your new home.

ON THE VIRGE... The Journey of a Lifetime

© 2018 KNIGHTsong Enterprises, Joe KNIGHT, Greenville TX, www.joeknight.us

ISBN 978-1975958411

COVER PHOTOGRAPHY AND ARTWORK

© 2018 KNIGHTsong Ministries, Joe KNIGHT, Greenville TX, www.joeknight.us

TABLE OF CONTENTS...

INTRODUCTION...

Part travelogue, part devotional, all adventure. Join us as we head out together ON THE VIRGE, The Journey of a Lifetime.

Matt was all of nine years old when Shaunda and I were married. Even though I had been a Pastor for nearly all of my career and involved in public ministry since I was eleven years old, divorce would ravage my family. Entirely through the grace of God however, God would restore my life and allow me to complete my career in Church ministry without ever missing a Sunday. If you think that sounds like a miracle to you, consider what a miracle that was in the mid 1990's. I was raising my own two children on my own when I met Matt's mom. That "restoration" for me included a Godly wife and her "package deal" that included her three children. Matt was one of those three.

Shaunda and I would soon discover that blending a family would be one of the most difficult challenges of our lives. Being in the ministry tended to complicate the matter even further. No complaints here, only a statement of facts. Even though I served a group of amazing people through the last twenty one years of my Church ministry, being a preacher's kid can stilll be tough. Lynn and Joey had grown up in it. Jodi, Matt and Brian were thrown into it. The pressures and expectations can be difficult, and all of us had to struggle with it at one time or another, all, that is, except Matt. He embraced it.

Matt was a tremendous young athlete. When he was a preteen however, he unexpectedly expressed an interest in music. I was quite pleased and made certain that everyone knew that he inherited that from "my side of the family". This interest in music soon transformed into an all out call to ministry when he was a young teenager. From that moment on, Matt seemed singularly commited to a career as a Pastor.

Matt went on to earn a full scholarship to Jacksonville Baptist College, gaining an associates degree. He then earned a scholarship to Criswell College. At Christmas break in that third year of his college, Matt was diagnosed with Non-Hodgkins Lymphoma, a brutal cancer that would ravage his body and ultimately take his life, and bring his ministry to an untimely end.

Words fail to describe the heartache and pain that this loss brought to our family. I chronicled this Journey and the incredible return of hope to our lives in TEARS IN A BOTTLE, LESSONS FROM A BROKEN HEART. After writing the book, I programmed an entire worship service to tell his story. In 2012, three years after Matt's death, this worship service became the vehicle for the book release.

In the days after the book release, a strange stirring began to bubble in my soul. Could God use Matt's story in an even bigger way? Could his choice to worship God in the face of one of life's most difficult struggles be an inspiration to others? What if we went from church to church to tell this story?

I have always enjoyed travelling. As a young man, I toured for several years in a music group. You can read about that in STORIES FROM THE ROAD. As the children grew up and left home, Shaunda and I began to talk about "life after kids". We talked about hitting the road full time after retirement. We spoke of National Parks and the remote wilderness, of seeing and experiencing places we had only read about.

But what if these two dreams could somehow meet?

I vividly remember the day I came home from work and Shaunda used that tired, overworked phrase: "I've got good news and bad news. Which do you want first?"

Why the good news of course!

"Well", she continued, I've done the math (Shaunda is a number cruncher by trade) and we will have enough money to buy that class A diesel pusher you want".

"About time" I thought to myself. "I'm not getting any younger". And then it hit me and I blurted out: "What's the bad news?"

Shaunda responded: "The only problem is you'll be 88 years old."

Wow, talk about a dream killer! But then she continued…

"But, if you really want to do this, we could sell our house, buy a truck and a fifth wheel and live in it for two years.   During that time we could save enough money to give it a try for at least two years.

And with that, the dream began in earnest.   This work follows that dream from here, right up until the last months of this two-year JOURNEY OF A LIFETIME.

You can follow along with us, as it happened from the years of planning, through the amazing God moment on the way back from west Texas at the end of the two years.   That's the day when we realized that Matt's story had touched more than 10,000 people in person and countless thousands more through the book during these two years.

And that's also the day I realized that I had been completely wrong.   Matt's ministry did not end with his death.   He is still touching lives today.   Matt's life mattered… and it *still* does.

> ON THE VIRGE…   "The Virge", the nickname for Matt used by so many of his friends, and the name we lovingly assigned to our fifth wheel.

>> THE JOURNEY OF A LIFETIME… Our "once in a lifetime" opportunity to sell everything we had and hit the road to tell Matt's story and experience some of the amazing beauty of this country, and also to make the correlation to the Journey that *is* our lifetime.

Most of the chapters are followed by a section entitled THE GREATER JOURNEY.   I have added these sections in order to allow this work to serve as a devotional as well.

Part travelogue, part devotional, all adventure. Join us as we head out together ON THE VIRGE, THE JOURNEY OF A LIFETIME.

Learn about our ministry? Check out the KNIGHTsong Ministries website…
www.joeknight.us

Want to watch videos and experience even more? Check out our ON THE VIRGE playlist…
https://tinyurl.com/ON-THE-VIRGE

Part 1
The Winds of Change

CHAPTER 1
Thirty-One

TIME TO "GET OUT OF DODGE"

Like many Americans my age (and even quite a few younger than I by way of "re-run"), I grew up with Gunsmoke. There's nothing like an evening (or now an afternoon) with Doc, Kitty and Festus. Even though you could count on Marshall Matt Dillon being out of town for a good portion of the show, you could likewise count on him returning just in time to save the day at the last possible moment. There might also be an instant when the Marshall would give the dreaded ultimatum to the rogue cowboy in the filthy, dark hat: "Get out of Dodge" would come the warning. A phrase that still lingers in our daily discourse.

Who would have ever dreamed that where I am today may mark the beginning of yet another giant dream. I have been told that the only real difference between a young man and an old man is found in his ability to dream. There have been times when a dream of any description was difficult for me to perceive. Heartaches come and strangle the life out of our dreams. Anger short circuits the process that creates dreams. Circumstances can cause us to nearly give up completely; and when we do, along with our withering spirit dies the dream.

I sit at the back end of my best "earning years". I am not a wealthy man by anyone's standards, but I have also never been "forsaken" by my Mighty God either. And when it is, by conventional wisdom at least, nearly time to "wrap things up, downscale and purchase a comfortable rocker", I have the awesome privilege of dreaming at least one more grand dream. There is no guarantee that this dream will ever get off the ground. If you are reading this, however, that is a pretty good indication that it did. At the writing of this chapter I am sitting squarely on the backside of my fifties. If things go as planned I will be into my sixties before this work is complete. As a matter of fact yet again, if things go as planned, it will be thirty one months from this writing before the journey ever even begins. Then again, our Journeys in life seldom really began when we thought they would; and things rarely went as we planned.

When I was a very young man, after a few years as a "travelling troubadour" of sorts, I took a position as Music Director at my home church. After a year there, eighteen months at a second Church in Ohio, four years in Decatur Illinois and nearly eight years in Springfield Missouri, I came to Greenville Texas. At the time of this writing I have served there nearly 19 years. Add all that up and add and subtract a few months here and there you will see that I have served as a Pastor for more than 31 years at the time of this writing.

STRESS OR DON'T STRESS, DREAM OR DON'T DREAM
I have come to believe that a great deal of the stress in our lives is brought about when two completely

opposite, yet forceful opinions, beliefs or ideas exist in our conciousness (or perhaps even in our subconciousness) at the same time. For example, when a young person really "loves" someone, yet remaining loyal to a parent requires leaving that love unrequited, inevitably stress is a byproduct. Or perhaps when we know that doing the right thing means saying "no" when all within us wants to say "yes", we struggle again with a war in our spirit that robs us of personal peace.

In my career path in the Ministry, knowing when to accept a call to serve a Church is a decision that is likewise often frightening and confusing; and often stressful. Other times it is quite obviously the thing to do and is met with nothing but excitement and anticipation. Leaving a call is similar. I'm afraid that my current experience is more in line with the former than the latter. I love my church, and I believe they love me as well. For no seemingly logical reason I began to believe last Fall that it might be time for me to move on. As time progressed till now (Fall, one year later), circumstances have borne out that lead me to believe that to be just the case.

When you are young and energetic, a season of impending change can be quite exhilarating. When you find yoursef not so young and not so energetic it can border a bit more on terrifying. Large parts of me scream "no, no! Stay put at all cost, take no risks, secure your financial future while you still have the chance." The other half screams equally as loudly; "chase the dream, don't roll over yet, there are still roads to travel, adventures to be lived, dreams to be dreamed.

Well there it is, two completely opposite yet forceful opinions, beliefs and ideas existing at the same time; and believe me, that creates stress.

Enter into the dilemma a piece of the puzzle unexpected and equally unwelcome, yet quite unavoidable. Seems that the decision to "stay and finish" no longer remains an option in my heart. Presented with "start over in a new place" or the "chasing of the dream"; the decision became much easier. Yet, I still find great displeasure and the accompanying "stress" brought about by those "completely opposite yet forceful opinions".

The decision I face now is far simpler; dream or don't dream. If I dream, I retain the ability to be a young man. If I cease to dream, the choice is made for me and I will pass quietly into the night, while slowly becoming an old man.

So there it is... the decision made, the terror begins. Yet the excitement of a new Journey lives right beside it.

WHY DO THIS?
So what is the dream? For those of you who have read TEARS IN A BOTTLE, you know a little of the road our Family has travelled through the loss of a child. For those of you who have not read it, please obtain a copy. In doing so, you become a part of today's Journey for us!

A great deal of the "making sense" part of the "Matt thing" for us, is found in telling his story. That process began with the writing of the book. It continued with the public book release in July of 2012. It has since manifested itself in radio interviews, concerts and speaking opportunities and soon a small group Bible Study. Simply stated, I take every opportunity to share Matt's story in every way and at every turn. I do this for several reasons. Selfishly, because it somehow strangely keeps him alive in some abstract way.

New folks have joined our church that neither knew Matt nor were led in worship by him, let alone watch his Journey unfold. There are others who marvelled at Matt, wept with Matt and watched the entirety of the Journey play out, often week to week, on the platform of our Church. They watched as cancer made its initial onslaught, only to be beaten back by determination and aggressive treatment; and they worshipped as Matt led "How Great Is Our God" , "Blessed Be Your Name" and "Healer". Many watched as remission turned to relapse and they looked in vain for Matt on the Sundays he was too ill to take the platform. Then they personally witnessed as he began to move perceptibly slower to the microphone and led "Mighty To Save" and "You Never Let Go". We all sat back and watched Matt's hairline and waistline go through drastic changes. We watched his color change from "normal" to yellow and then to pale white. We listened while a strong, vibrant young voice turned weak and crackly; while trained, disciplined hands began to fumble for chords as chemo took its toll on Matt's thought process.

Physically, Matt went through enormous changes. Yet the "power in this picture" was found in the fact that Matt's testimony and unyielding love for Christ never wavered at all; through it all. Each Sunday morning, when physically able, found him guitar in hand, leading worship, then sitting on a stool in front of his Middle School students. Then one day, not at all unexpected, hundreds gathered for the singular worship service that neither Matt nor I would attend. I never missed one worship opportunity during the entirety of the Journey... until that Sunday morning... that precious Sunday when early in the morning hours Matt escaped the body that had failed him and entered into the presence of the God who never did.

Yet many of those wonderful people have moved on. Most will never forget Matt, but rightfully so, few think of him on a regular basis. In some ways, his Mom and I have made a similar Journey. In other ways, we never will. So yes, unapologetically, I long to tell his story.

DO WHAT?
Add to this equation the undying memories of another young man so many years earlier touring the country in a thirty five foot bus with the smell of spent diesel fuel lingering in the air. Do the math and you will come up with the dream: What if we took the risk, sold the car and the house (and nearly everything in it), bought a pickup truck and a fifth wheel? We named the fifth wheel "The Virge". That was Matt's nickname for as long as I can remember. What if we left it all behind to live full time on the road and seek out every opportunity, paid and unpaid, to tell Matt's story?

Crazy? Perhaps.
Frightening? Absolutely!

Yet, the fear of losing the ability to dream is to me more frightening still.

THE WHO, WHAT, WHY, WHERE AND WHEN.
Who?
Shaunda and me.

What?
We put the house on the market, sell my small, towable Ford Escape (that's a different story that "started before the start") and buy a truck and fifth wheel, and lovingly name it "The Virge".

Why?
To tell Matt's story.

Where?
"North to Alaska" by way of anywhere I can share the story.

When?
Thirty one months from now… on March 6, 2016
So there you have it… we plan to get *on* "The Virge" and get *out* of "Dodge".

On the Virge… the Journey of a Lifetime.

THE GREATER JOURNEY...

Read Genesis 12:1-5

I would never presume to compare the faith required for this "Journey of a Lifetime" to that required of Abraham. There are however, some similarities. With those in mind, consider this...

> *1. What would you do if you believed God had called you from your family, your hometown and your friends?*

> *2. What if He were sending you to a place where you didn't know anyone?*

> *3. Was Abraham promised a reward for his faith?*

> *4. Is there any part of "Getting out of Dodge" that appeals to you? If so, why do you think it does?*

Thought for the day...
So you think you're too old for such a Journey with God? How old was Abraham? Here's a hint: He was a lot older than I was.

CHAPTER 2
Just The Facts Ma'am

You guessed it, another cheesy 60's television reference. You could count on Sergeant Joe Friday (badge number 714) cutting through all the baloney and getting directly to the details surrounding the crime and its usual conclusion that would fill a 30-minute television show. After several curt comments and emotionless interviews with stereotypical citizens, we would all know the practical pertinent details. That's what this chapter is about. Are you ready? Here it comes; just the facts.

I was on board emotionally long before Shaunda. Such a drastic change in lifestyle however would require a unified commitment of husband and wife. If that was never achieved, at least I could buy a smaller RV.

At some time in the distant past we started talking about retirement (at some point in the distant future) and hitting the road to do some travelling. The talk got rather serious while on our "Route 66" road trip in the spring of 2010. That trip was envisioned as our "kid's are all raised, we've got a little time (and finally a little cash) for ourselves, let's put it all into perspective, let's relive America's glorious past (while I relive a similar childhood journey)" trip. You can read more about that trip in STORIES FROM THE ROAD... Lessons From Life and Death.

After several leisurely days meandering down the Mother Road while eating at diners and staying in vintage hotels, we literally stumbled across a free classic car show. After perusing aisle after aisle of vintage automobiles, muscle cars and even an original Batmobile, we came upon one of the coolest forms of transportation I had ever seen. It was a restored full sized original Ford Bronco towing a 1960's vintage travel trailer painted to match. The interior of the trailer was decorated entirely in Route 66 memorabilia, right down to Route 66 window coverings and Route 66 upholstery.

Almost simultaneously we looked at each other and said out loud, nearly in unison... "We could do that!"... And the dream was born.

Over the next months the dream was cultivated by a myriad of conversations and even a few "what if we dids" and an occasional "we could always". Both of us became very excited about a new adventure in life. More than a few memories of life on the road as a teenager travelling the highways and back roads of this great country in that 40 foot greyhound bus, soon assured the dream would bloat into a Diesel pusher class A towing a small SUV.

In the spring of 2011 it was time to test drive the dream. Empowered by the graciousness of an unselfish church member who donated the use of their 37-foot Class A motorhome, we were off. We planned a 6-day jaunt to Branson Missouri by way of Hot Springs Arkansas.

I sat down (comfortably and confidently I might add) behind the wheel of a really nice, really large, really borrowed motorhome. It had been more than a few years since I drove that old silver and red bus, but the technique quickly came back to me and we were off.

While I was rolling down the highway imagining myself several financial classes above reality enjoying the "really big" and "really nice" parts, Shaunda was sitting in the co-pilot's seat concentrating on the "really borrowed" part.

I'm not certain if it was her silence or her strange "greenish" complexion that first gained my attention. It may have even been the only occasionally audible prayer. It might have been the death grip on the armrest that turned her hands pure white. At any rate, I finally realized that the moments I spent lost in my younger days corresponded with her moments of sheer terror that were the precursor of an epic meltdown to come.

Long story short... rainy weather, borrowed coach, too many curves and mountain roads equals one vacation cut short.

OK... enough about that. If I were to write it and Shaunda were to find it, that would be the end of a perfectly good dream!

As Paul Harvey used to say, here's the rest of the story. After that trip we didn't even talk about the dream for a year. Occasionally I'd turn my head to watch a shiny, sleek double axle Class A motorhome roar by. I would then find myself confronted with the same response I would expect if it had been an attractive young lady half my age.

Then came the day when I least expected to discuss such things. "I've been thinking" Shaunda began the conversation, "that I may have allowed my fears to make me pass up one of the greatest adventures of my lifetime. Could I have another chance?"

"You bet", I answered rather quickly.

Game on. The "thirty-one month thing" was the result of a little thought, a little consideration of the seasons and some simple mathematical equations.

Leaving a steady employment and striking out into unknown territory is a level of risk to which I have not often entered. One of the first considerations was given to my coming years. At the time of this writing, (month 1 of the 31), I am 56 years old. Who knows what the future holds.

Thirty years of ministry and thirty years of parenting have left me with uncertainty that creates a quandary. I share similar concerns with many others at this stage of the life. Through the years I have watched people work until their social security dictated retirement age, only to suffer a heart attack or other debilitating illness that put an immediate end to their dreams. Still others work until their life ends for lack of any dream at all. I have met others who retired much earlier or even a bit later than my current age and find themselves bored or unchallenged. Most significantly I watched my 22 year old son breathe his last breath with the majority of his dreams never realized (That's the "TEARS IN A BOTTLE... Lessons From A Broken Heart" thing).

Here's my dilemma...   I don't want to retire too early and run out of money or dreams... or both. I don't want to retire too late and not have the health or time to enjoy the journey.

Years ago I chose the ministry path instead of the music path. No one (especially me) knows whether the "other" path would have been more lucrative, but it certainly held a significantly greater possibility. Please don't read any disappointment or bitterness into this because I assure you that none exists. I would not trade my life for any other even if I could. It's just that the reality in the path I chose, barring scandalous behavior, assured me of a bit less on the remuneration side. As such, I have no large 401K, IRA or pension plan in place. The financial "when" is a calculation of when I might have an acceptable combination of emergency fund road stake and safety net. That number is 28 months into the 31.

The conclusion of 28 months places me in December of 2015. January and February of 2016 are months 29 and 30. The first Sunday in March of 2016 will mark my 21st anniversary at Family Fellowship. Should the Lord allow me to reach that goal, I would be 58 years old and in my 34th year of full time ministry, and that would be month 31.

That's the simplicity of the decision. However, when you add to that the emotion and the intense prayer, it really was a great deal deeper and more complicated than it sounds here. In the spirit of the "31 month" concept, I created a reasonable "to do list" to track the plan and reach the dream.

And as it usually does... life happened.

THE GREATER JOURNEY...

Read 2 Peter 1:4

Study each of the following verses from the book of Matthew. Read them in context and see if you can determine the promise associated with each given.

> *Matthew 6:33*
> *Matthew 16:25*
> *Matthew 19:29*

Thought for the day...
How dare we say sacrifice when we give up anything for Him who gave up everything?
Romans 12:1

CHAPTER 3
What A Difference A Day Makes

Or to be more honest, what a difference three days make. A history lesson may one day teach us that I was correct in assuming that the fall of 2013 was a short lived real estate bubble in East Texas. A history lesson may also teach us that I was wrong in assuming that it was time to market our family home. In either case, it doesn't really matter because our decision to sell most certainly now is a part history.

A quick question to a dear friend and our financial advisor after one of our early Monday morning Bible studies yielded an equally quick answer. My financial advisor knew about my long term dreams not because he was my advisor, but rather because he was my friend.

"Should I begin to market my house now or wait until next spring"?

There it was; a simple question. I realize that no one can see the future, move time and space, let alone predict a volatile Country's financial future. At any rate, his worst guess stood a far greater chance of being more "right" than my best one.

"Do it now" came the simple answer.

To be honest, I don't ask for advice all that often. It seems that many of the times I was asked for "advice" were really only a disguised request for my blessing. As a matter of practice I only ask for advice when I am unsure of a decision and when I am willing to take the advice given. A quick and early lunch with my wife consisted of some great chips and dip along with a great new recipe for some light guacamole, and some pretty heavy conversation to go with it. By the end of that short lunch we determined to follow the advice I had sought out.

I phoned a friend who worked as a real estate broker. An evening of pouring over figures, comps and several other factors concluded with a discussion of property valuation. Any history with "sellers" would certainly remind you that we always feel like what we have is worth more than it really is.

A patient friend crunched the numbers and determined what our house might bring on the open market. A combination of courtesy and hope led her to arrive at a number a good deal higher yet. From that number she subtracted comissions, fees, taxes... you get it. Finally came the best case bottom line.

I was approaching this transaction from an entirely different direction. I wanted to come out of the deal with enough cash to make our dream work. I started with my bottom line and then added her figures to it. My number was as you might guess, quite a bit higher yet!

Some grace on her part met the unreasonable expectations on mine and we agreed on a listing price.

My wife and I signed our names, and that was it. No pressure though. Such an unrealistically high asking price would no doubt buy us nothing more than a guarantee of a long listing period. With that came plenty of time to prepare.

It was nearly October. The Holidays were right around the corner, Our oldest daughter was getting married in three weeks. And remember that really neat fifth wheel that was a part of the master plan? It was in the shop for an extended time with yet more warranty issues.

But, no pressure. These things take time.

How much time? Three days, ten days, thirty days,

Three days after listing we got the asking price that guaranteed our bottom line. Ten days after listing we were closed and funded. Thirty days and the majority of our earthy posessions would need to be sold or stored and we would be on the street.

The dream seems as if it is about to take on a life of its own.

THE GREATER JOURNEY...

Read 2 Corinthians 5:17

Study Isaiah 55:8-12
Are you really ready to follow Christ wherever He leads? What about whenever He leads?

Christianity is not now, nor has it ever been about fitting God into our culture, thought processes and goals. It is about an inward new creation that fits into His.

Thought for the day...
Am I really a new creation in Christ or merely a Christian of convenience?

CHAPTER 4
Fifteen

Wow, who would have ever imagined that the "dream" would have such "long legs"? Here I sit, a year and a quarter since I last touched this work. I find myself in a local state park with leaves falling all around me (literally) while listening to Christmas Music. Granted it is the end of October and the predicted record high tomorrow is 90 degrees. (For all of you "Christmas People" like me, Christmas music comes out October 1, Christmas books on November 1. It's OK, go for it!). At any rate, here I am... month 15 of 31.

We started by paring down our posessions to only retain those we "had to have" to live and several small items considered irreplacable. After a few months of learning to live in our newly aquired small space we pared down again... and then yet again. Amazing how much we just "had to have" that we didn't really need at all.

Did I mention "small space"? How about 396 square feet small? We have been in our "small space" for just a few days under one year, and the lessons have been manifold and regular! Little things like "water freezes in the winter" and "propane bottles always run out in the middle of the night" to name a couple.

K~S~

A year earlier when our house sold so quickly it was time to bring Shaunda's Mom and Step Dad into our confidence. They owned a home situated on eight acres just outside of our hometown. With no crops to tend to or cows to feed, water or keep up with, we thought they might enjoy a son-in-law. The day soon came when a breakfast opportunity at the local eatery afforded itself. It seemed like the right time to inform them that the man who was responsible for their daughter's well being would soon sucessfully render her homeless. They would also learn that soon they could add unemployed to his description.

A quick jab of the shocking information interspersed with some eggs, biscuits and gravy brought about some deafening silence and awkward glances between the now shocked parents. Really? Had the fact of our house being sold and having less than a month to vacate been an overload? Add to that the fact that our new "condo on wheels" was still in the shop. I know that this idea must have sounded a bit "off the wall".

After a few days, I mean seconds, of silence, another slice of bacon and the accompaning difficult swallow, it seemed that Forrest Gump, I mean Dean, was about to speak. After sharing my "secret" my Father-in-Law responded: "I guess it's time to tell you what we're planning". Soon Shaunda and I were let into another "secret".

"We're selling our house also and splitting the acreage in half, moving into our fifth wheel on the remaining four acres. Ever heard of Volunteer Christian Builders?"

Yes I had. And now it was *my* jaw on the floor. They were in their mid seventies. How could anyone be so impulsive and reckless as to sell their house and move into a fifth wheel? Never mind, scratch that.

I have been told that the difference between a young man and an old man is found in his ability to dream. Let life's circumstances beat you, and you run out of dreams. Then you become an old man regardless of how many years you have lived. I have also learned that the key to longevity in a career, relationship or any venture for that matter is found in the ability to reinvent ourselves. When one door closes, or you close it yourself; instead of quitting or wallowing in debilitating self pity you rather attempt to find a different door.

Here I was in my mid fifties lamenting my later life changes and I come face to face with a man twenty years my senior doing essentially the same thing. Old man you say? I say not at all. Age seems to have little to do with how old you are.

After I picked up my jaw (and my bacon) off the floor realizing I had not come even close to winning the day with my paltry announcement, Shaunda and I found ourselves invited to be a part of their dream in establishing a home base for all of our adventures.

And so began the first "life of it's own" adventure. Soon I would go back to "school". I am a musician, Pastor and Police Officer. I am not a carpenter, electrician or plumber (nor painter nor farmer; you get the picture). Yet here I was, remodling a "shotgun" barn apartment, installing 50 amp electrical service in two locations on a piece of property, running a trencher, installing fresh water lines and septic lines, painting, spreading gravel and a dozen other things I had been gleefully ignorant of only a dozen weeks earlier.

Thankfully, my Father-in-Law is a good and patient teacher; perhaps a much better teacher than I was a learner. Why he even taught me the two things I needed to know to be a plumber:

Payday is Friday, and... Disregard the latter, this is a G-rated adventure. Sorry plumbers. my Father-in-Law though quite wise, doesn't speak for everyone.

THE GREATER JOURNEY...

Read Luke 14:25-30

In this passage certainly Jesus was not at all speaking of those who would take off on a Journey like ours. Yet in verse 28 He lays out a pretty good thought concerning forward planning. He speaks about counting the cost before you start the building process.

Thought for the day...
What long term goal do you have for yourself? Your family? Your work? Or are you living in the moment, just trying to get from day to day. Do these goals fall in line with the character of Christ?

What are you doing, or perhaps begin to do to plan ahead for these goals? Can you start today? This moment?

CHAPTER 5
Hard To Say Goodbye

Through the myriad of cost cutting measures, somehow we were actually able to meet our financial goal. That process actually became a game. One example? Sure!

We all but stopped eating in restaurants. On Friday mornings (my day off at Church) we often headed to another town just west of us that had a popular warehouse store. Between those two points there is, however, a certain restaurant chain that has a $2, $4, $6, $8 menu. They offer a breakfast offering at each price point. Seems like a good enough reason to make an exception.

Here was the routine: Get up, make two cups of coffee in "to go" cups. Make a stop at that inexpensive restaurant where we traded off weeks. One week I would get to order off the $4 menu, Shaunda would order off the $2, and we would split our meals. Drinking only water, we were soon out the door for $6 (plus tax and tip) where the remainder of our coffee awaited us, still hot. I tell you that saving money became a game, and it was fun.

Many small pieces of our lives turned to the Journey as well. Since we had liquidated nearly all our posessions and we were living on the Virge in 396 square feet, family and friends began complaining that there was nothing to get us as gifts for Christmas and birthdays. Keep in mind that the years of preparation saw to several of these. Our answer? Gift cards. In addition to saving up the cash, we would leave town with gift cards representing a few dozen meals and several tanks of fuel. I tell you it was fun!

All the while that the excitement was building toward our launch date, my heart was also filling with the growing reality that I would be leaving the church I had served for more than half of my career, over twenty years. Talk about mixed emotions.

Saying goodbye is never easy, but it can be extra difficult when you spend your life in the ministry. Now the ministry can be defined in several ways. For me, being a Pastor has always had as much to do with what goes on "off the platform" as it does with what goes on "on the platform". It is about being involved in the lives of people and being available and interested when their lives are in crisis. In case it hasn't dawned on you, engaging people at this level can have an unexpected consequence; you discover you have learned to love them. And that makes saying goodbye infinitely more difficult.

The timing surrounding my leaving Family Fellowship was a little unique as well. I wanted our church to be a part of this journey, so I tried to be very transparent. I gave my Pastor a two year notice. I told the church almost exactly one year in advance. This made things easier, and more difficult all at the same time.

The last year held for me some really great worship experiences, and some amazing times of fellowship with the people in our worship ministry. I had the opportunity to close out 2015 with a wonderful Christmas concert. And then the calendar caught up with me. March 6 was right around the corner.

The worship service on my last Sunday was pretty typical in structure. I intentionally programmed my personal favorites for that final day and ended with How Great Is Our God. There was a reception in our honor in the Fellowship Hall after second service. No one had eaten lunch yet so this event was certain to be brief. I was good with that. This whole "mixed emotions" thing was taking its toll on me.

Near the end of those few moments of fellowship together, a man about my age stepped up and shook my hand. He was not a musician, but rather an excellent cabinent maker. He also excelled in technical areas including audio and video. He was involved in the worship ministry when I arrived at this church, twenty one years earlier on this very day. We still worked together.

He smiled at me and I smiled in return. He looked me directly in the eyes and said: "Right now I don't remember a single song you sang..."

I must admit that I was taken aback by his opening comments. I sure was anxious to see how he finished them.

"But I *do* remember" he continued, "that when my daughter had a car accident you came to the hospital to see her between services. Not sure I ever said thank you."

He had just given me a priceless gift. He acknowledged with his words that I had achieved my desire as a Pastor. I have long believed that being a Pastor is not a position to be attained, it is rather a relationship to be earned. Yet it is those "relationships attained" that make saying "goodbye" so hard.

> *Sometimes its hard to say "goodbye",*
> *To the friends we've known so well.*
> *We've made memories to keep,*
> *We've got so many things to tell.*
>
> *As we follow God's command,*
> *Leading through this promised land,*
> *Please forgive me if I cry,*
> *It's just so hard to say "goodbye".*

GOODBYE Words and Music by Joe KNIGHT © 1988 by KNIGHTsong Enterprises

CHAPTER 6
The First Rattle

Here we go... first "rattle out of the box" on our "Journey of a Lifetime" and *nothing is going as planned.*

So what did we have planned? How about a few days in Tyler (a little more than an hour away to enjoy time with our granddaughter on her spring break) and then off to what Shaunda ordered? So what did Shaunda order? She asked for the first month to be reserved for R&R in a place with no cell phones. Enter into the conversation: Big Bend.

Between planning and implementation of "the plan" our oldest daughter Jodi informed us that Keegan Matthew was on the way (oh yeah, he's named after that other guy) right in the middle of our first tour. This offered a very welcome and wonderful alteration to our planning I might add. So we opted for the first few days in Tyler for spring break duties, then on to Big Bend for a month, then back to Tyler for introductions, and then back to the first tour.

Our last day in Tyler before leaving for Big Bend included a trip to the Doctor for Jodi, accompanied by her very excited mom, Shaunda. That led to the hospital, and tests, and contractions, then bed rest, then the likelihood for a delivery that seemed would be much sooner than later. How does that affect us? Please let me illustrate.

Instead of looking at this:

I am still looking at this:

Instead of sitting in a remote desert, mountain gazing during the day and star gazing at night, I am waxing my truck in a 20' wide slot in a very public RV park while our granddaughter is at school.

Now wait a minute, is this really all that bad?

While "wax on, wax off" consumed my morning with a mind numbing routine, courtesy of the RETRO playlist on my iPod, I received great inspiration from a 1970's philosopher (who, by the way was actually inspired by a far greater philosopher whether he ever realized it or not)

> *To everything, turn turn turn*
> *There is a season, turn, turn turn,*

And then I smiled as I realized that at some point in the future I will most likely drink in that desert landscape, and it will most likely look exactly the same as it does now.

The second picture on the other hand will never again present itself quite like it did today. It will all too soon be gone altogether; and with it will be swept away a thousand memories.

And then I remembered last week. My beautiful eight-year-old granddaughter and me... hand in hand dancing around the pool, her laughter echoing from every corner of the metal indoor pool enclosure. In my heart I can still hear her say, "Oh Poppi, I love you. I wish every Friday could be like this". (Yes, she really said that, and no, I will never forget it). Soon she'll be home from school and we'll be off to the pool again. (Sorry about all that homework mom).

And then I'm reminded of a lesson from another Journey: *Never take one moment for granted.*

So here we go... first "rattle out of the box" on our "Journey of a Lifetime" and *EVERYTHING is going as planned.*

THE GREATER JOURNEY...

King Solomon was dealing with a crisis of his own. As a very wealthy and wise man he learned the futility of life when measured by earthly standards. In Ecclesiastes 3:1, he wrote the following words:

> *There is a time for everything, and a season for every activity under the heavens:*

Thought for the day...
Can God be a party to the "waiting rooms" of our lives? Has His timing ever contradicted your plans? How did you deal with the disappointment? Was the ultimate outcome of the waiting for your "good"?

Perhaps you can't honestly answer those questions because you find yourself in a waiting time right now. Can God be trusted even when our plans are frustrated? Can YOU trust Him? Now?

Now read Proverbs 13:12. What can we learn about waiting from this verse also written by Solomon?

CHAPTER 7
What a Day

Wow, another day stuck in Tyler. What a day.

- I did not wake up early to a high desert landscape with the sun peeking through feathery clouds.

- I did not ride my mountain bike miles into a desert paradise.

- I did not feel the warmth of the Hot Springs of Big Bend National Park.

- I did not hold gaze across the Rio Grande and wonder what amazing secrets were held in it's yesterday.

- I did not view the starry heavens from a remote "dark sky" location.

What a day.

- I did however wake up early to be a special guest at 2nd grade grandparent's day.

- I did however ride miles all around this crazy city going from school to hospital and back while precious cargo sang sweet worship songs loudly in the back seat.

- I did feel the warmth of a tiny hand slip into mine during school chapel.

- I did gaze on six pounds of a living, breathing slice of brand new life that Lord willing, may also one day call me "Poppi".

- I did realize that you don't need to have dark skies to see heaven. I spent the day surrounded by it. I just needed to open my eyes.

Wow, another day stuck in Tyler. What a day!

THE GREATER JOURNEY...

Read Psalm 73. Ever struggle with the fact that sometimes, or sometimes quite often, bad people seem to get away with doing bad things? Seems you're in good company. A guy named Asaph obviously struggled with the same thing. And of little real value, but something I found interesting, this guy was known as an eminent singer.

Thought for the day...
Read Psalm 73:17 once again.
    "...till I entered the sanctuary of God; then I understood their final destiny."

Can you see the vast difference that a "God view" of life and a focus on eternity can make in our perspective? Are you ready to accept the reality that when we ask God to change our circumstances He often rather chooses to change our perspective of those circumstances?

CHAPTER 8
Listen To The Rhythm

As my wife Shaunda often asks: "Does everything always have to be a song with you?" Well, kind of.

So here I sit by myself in our "home on wheels". Shaunda is at the Doctor's Office with Keegan Matthew (oh yeah, and his mom) for his first checkup. After two weeks in the NICU and five days at home, once again the world appears wonderfully bright and different, thanks to a change in perspective. Oh yeah, while I write I listen to the rhythm of the falling rain.

Time to check the air pressure, tighten the lug nuts, crank down the TV antenna, hook up the trailer, dump the tanks... wait, TMI, I know. (Something I also hear from Shaunda on a fairly regular basis.) Guess it's finally time to leave.

I'm not certain why I cry at weddings (and funerals and graduations and songs I haven't heard since high school and old John Wayne movies), but I think they may all have one specific thing in common. It may be that they all involve the end of one thing and the beginning of another. Why is it that it seems that life itself tends to teach us over and over that we must say "goodbye"?

I have had the amazing privilege of standing in front of two of my children and lead them in the exchanging of their vows with their respective spouses. As they looked longingly into each other's eyes, they saw only tomorrows. I stood in the same place at the same time listening to the same thing, but I saw yesterdays as well. While their eyes filled with tears at the prospects of future joys… my eyes misted too, at the memories of days now long gone never to be experienced again.

Somehow though, I was transported back through time where I once again found myself in a small backyard on a warm spring day. I was with a small boy; two ball gloves and a single piece of privacy fence. The latter was intended to shield an unsightly view of the propane tank, but it more practically served as an awesome backstop to rein in the not so occasional errant knuckle ball. "I do" shocked me back to the reality at hand, and my two-second trip to yesterday was over. "Hello" to a new world of adventure is exciting. Goodbyes are hard. Life tends to give you both, often at the same time.

Similar emotions can grip us when we spend hours in a school auditorium or high school football field agonizing through a seemingly unending list of names waiting to hear that one special name announced. That one name that represents to us a milestone, a success, a whirlwind transition from one chapter of life to another. A wonderful hello, and a painful goodbye; and all at precisely the same moment.

Often a familiar melody or signature musical idiom can return feelings and memories we thought long forgotten. Musicians call that a "hook", and for good reason.

And laugh if you will, but knowing what an icon like John Wayne meant to my generation, take a moment and watch "The Shootist" one more time. It is no doubt true that this actor relied on his stature, persona and one-liners for success. But look deeply into his eyes in this the final movie of his life. Many believe that John Wayne delivered more raw emotion in these 90 minutes than in the entirety of his other movies combined.

Understand that he made this movie about an aging gunfighter dying with cancer after he himself had already lost one lung to the same disease. Note that he missed several days of scheduled filming because of illness. Realize that less than two years from the release of this movie, his last film, he would succumb to that disease.

Factor all these things, and then listen to his heartrending line that may surpass all of his others combined. When confronted by Bond Rogers (Lauren Bacall) about his life as a gunfighter and cursed for the pain he had brought into their family, he was accused of being many things. He answered simply "I'm a dying man, scared of the dark".

I'm not convinced that John Wayne was ever a prizefighter, an Admiral, a Sergeant on Iwo Jima, a gunfighter, a US Calvary captain, and Indian fighter or a boxer. I'm pretty certain he never sought a real stagecoach for transportation, fought at the Alamo or bought an enormous cattle ranch outside of a town named after him. I doubt he could throw a ten-gallon hat onto a weather vane just once, let alone in repeated succession. As a matter of fact, I'm not certain he was all of anything he purported himself to be on the silver screen. Then again, that was his job. He was an actor.

I do believe however, that he truly knew what it meant to be a "dying man, scared of the dark". I also truly believe that is why the look in his eyes and expression on his face mirrored the words from his lips.

And with that movie John Wayne said goodbye.

"The Shootist" performed somewhat dismally at the box office. But I believe this is true because no one understood at the time the incredible significance this film held.

To drag the western theme out for one more painful moment… I've come a long way around the campfire to get where I'm going. Today, God willing, we get to pick up our eight year old Granddaughter after school one final time. Tonight we share supper with Jodi, Ben, Makenna and Keegan (although he won't be sharing much of what we're eating). And then we'll gather all our belongings and share a few awkward moments waiting for someone to say that awful word… that word that all these things have in common.

Even though we are a Pastor's family, believe me, we have known our share of tough goodbyes. Not every time we have parted company have the circumstances been pleasant. Seems these "goodbyes" typically involve tears, although they are not always "good" tears. Hmmm… Perhaps that's why I think of the participants at those weddings as ten year olds and not young adults.

I know that this one will involve tears… they've already started. I'm just trying not to short out my computer. These however, will all be "good tears". Bad memories are distant, good memories abound. Talk about the Grace of God. It hasn't always been that way.

As I write however, I am reminded of a series of "goodbyes" with my Mother so many years ago. She developed cancer when my children were of pre-school age. Courtesy of a wonderful pastor (Thank you Rev. Glenn Stockton) I was able to see my mother every month for the last 7 months of her life.

Early in my ministry, I took a position in a Church about seven hours from where I was raised. Pastor Stockton called me in his office in early January right after my mom was diagnosed, and he said something like this: "You will have a great career in the Ministry Joe, and you will serve many churches and many people… you will, however, only have one mother."

And with that he made the way clear for me to go home one weekend a month for "as long as my mother lived". That is exactly what I did. And for the record, as I sit here now nearly 30 years after my Mother's death, do you think I do not still feel an unbelievable debt to this man?

In my Mom's last months, she forbade us to say the word "goodbye". It was replaced, at her direction, by "so long". The occasional "slip of the tongue" guaranteed a reprimand fitting for the six-year boy she somehow always perceived me to be. Seems she also understood the finality of "goodbye" and the accompanying tears. For those months we always said "so long". In my Mother's rationalization, that meant that we would see each other again.

"Goodbye" was final. "So long" was not.

You may have already guessed this, but on the day that my Mother's body lay at the front of the small funeral chapel surrounded by flowers (that I can still smell right now), it finally was my turn to pass by. And I said... you guessed it... "So long Mom". For I know that I will see my mother once again. And what's more, she now knows Matt. I'm certain they have gotten acquainted and perhaps even swapped stories.

By the way, the same was true on that cool March morning when I stood by Matt's casket at the graveside. No "goodbye" then either...only "so long".

I am learning that one of the difficult elements of this "Journey" thing is the constant leaving. I served twenty-one years at one church making some of the greatest friends of my life... and then we leave. We share some amazing moments with a Church family in Eureka Springs, Arkansas, and then we leave. We get to know some great people at a little cowboy church in Joshua, Texas. We eat together and pray together and then we leave. We gather with a group of people at a tiny church at a mere crossroads in West Texas where we are surrounded by nothing but oil wells, cotton fields and blue sky. We sing, we share... and then we leave.

Our children are grown and spread out around the country. When Shaunda and I began talking about this Journey more than three years ago, we laid out some basic goals. If this "Journey of a Lifetime" really worked out, we figured we might actually get to spend *more* time with our children (and grandchildren) than we would during the occasional visits and vacations. While this was a privately shared dream of ours, we never could have believed that God would work things out like He has. Once again, talk about the Grace of God.

We came to Tyler Texas to enjoy five days with our Daughter, Son in Law and Granddaughter. Here we are, seven weeks later and we find ourselves in that "leaving" stage again. Only this time we are leaving a Daughter, a Son in Law, a Granddaughter…

And a Grandson.

Well, I've got this chapter about finished up, and guess what? The rain has stopped. The weatherman has promised sunny skies and warm weather to do that "hook up/dump the tanks" thing. (I know, still TMI).

So in a few hours we will once again have the opportunity to say…

So long.

All of life has a rhythm. There is a certain rhythm to the rain… as well as a certain rhythm as to when the rain stops and the bright sunshine appears again.

For we know that for those of us who know Christ, we will assuredly meet again. For you see, "goodbye" is not "really "goodbye" at all.   Talk about the Grace of God.

THE GREATER JOURNEY...

Do you ever cry at weddings? At graduations? At funerals? At all? Saying "goodbye" is part of life. Some say that the two inevitabilities in life are death and taxes. I have, however, seen some cheat the taxman and get away with it. No one has ever ultimately cheated death.   There is a second inevitable though.

Read Hebrews 9:26-28 and Romans 14:9-11.

Thought for the day... What if you were called to say your final goodbye, today? How do you feel about standing in front of a Holy God to give account for your failures and your sin?

Now read Romans 3:25.
Talk about the Grace of God!

Part 2
Chasing Spring

CHAPTER 9
Surprise!

Leaving Keegan in the capable hands of his Mother, we were off on our first real travel experience, and soon to the beginning of the public presentation of the story. "The story", more on that in a minute.

After a stop for a few wonderful days with more family in Latham Springs just south of Fort Worth, we hooked up once again and headed for New Mexico. The weatherman was promising an enhanced risk of tornadoes and large hail beginning just west of Fort Worth, so it made absolute sense to leave early and head west on I-20. Good thing we did. If we hadn't we wouldn't have been anywhere near Big Spring Texas when the storm front formed well west of where it was predicted. SURPRISE! Strong winds, hail, lighting and a dust storm... a dust storm??? I have much to learn about West Texas. We survived unscathed (and apparently so did "The Virge") while those back in Latham Springs were pelted... by nothing but rain.

After the storm we experienced (and I mean experienced) our first night of boondocking. For the inaugural experience, I chose a rest area in remote West Texas. There are many books, blogs and websites readily available concerning the dry camping experience, so I will only say that it was a wonderful and unique experience. For those of you who may be rank amateurs (like me), dry camping is defined as camping without any hookups. No water, no sewer, no electricity, be it in a dispersed campground, BLM land, alongside the road or in any large parking lot. Our 5th wheel is designed for just such an adventure, so this is not as terrifying as it initially sounds. Again I say it was a wonderful and unique experience.

It was wonderful because Shaunda and I experienced some of our first moments of real freedom on the road. We had a destination, but it would have required  traveling more than our self imposed daily mileage limit. Shaunda took her first full turn at "driving while pulling" so we arrived at this rest area well ahead of schedule...and that is another story entirely.

With a beautiful, clear, early spring West Texas sky, and the storms now well to the east, Shaunda fixed chef salads. We ate our supper at a nearly deserted picnic area watching the myriad of travelers and truckers zoom by on the interstate below. From our perspective we had no place to be, no schedule, no pressure...little stress.

And then we witnessed a gorgeous West Texas sunset.

And then it got unique.

It was unique because... because... because... never mind. I don't think I'll share that because... it's not fit for print. Don't go out too far on this one; it was neither criminal nor frightening... just unusual. I might clarify a bit by pointing out that my thirty plus years involved with law enforcement made this experience seem fairly mundane. Shaunda, on the other hand, ran to the window to watch the show. What show you ask? Never mind. Let's just say that it was unique, and that Shaunda should have ridden along with me a bit more often while I was on duty.

A dose of the "Long, Long Trailer" on the computer in our long, long trailer was followed by a truly unexpected good night's sleep. We awoke surrounded by trucks large enough to dwarf our 37 foot 5th wheel. Soon we were up and going again whistling a familiar Willie Nelson tune (yes, everything *is* a song).

Did I mention that this trip has cost us very little? When we moved into our RV for the two and one half years before our last Sunday at Family Fellowship, our children, family and friends asked us what they could get us for Christmases and birthdays. I guess it is quite difficult to give a gift to someone who is getting rid of much of what they already have. The perfect answer? Shaunda concluded: Gift cards.

When we left Family Fellowship, several of our members blessed us with gift cards and cash as well. Thank you! That's what we say every time we swipe a gift card at the diesel pump or cash goes on the table to pay for dinner. Hmmmm… Wonder if it will always be this easy?

Soon, with the interstate behind us, the "Welcome to New Mexico" sign assured us that we really were entering a new phase of the adventure. Driving past Hobbs and Carlsbad, we reached our destination in Lakewood New Mexico. We pulled into "The Ranch", an Escapees co-op park. (It will take you some Internet searching if you want to know what that is.) After being greeted warmly announced by the "ringing of the bell" (trust me here, full time rv'ers have a culture all their own) the camp host helped me back the Virge in our assigned spot.

By the way, I am going to write a conclusive book one day on how to successfully back a large 5th wheel. First however, I will learn to accomplish it without either of the "two d's": damage or domestic violence. I already have three years, several books and multiple teachers invested in the learning process and yet I find myself in the same dilemma I did when I first decided to take up the game of golf. Seems that no matter how much time and energy I invest, I just get worse. Don't search your favorite eBook site for this work anytime soon.

The Ranch is a different type of RV Park than you might expect. Rather than vacationers, this park is inhabited mostly by a group of people committed to the RV lifestyle who have taken up permanent or semi-permanent residency. Unoccupied lots are rented to other "club members". It is a really unique place…and not at all in the same way the rest area was unique. At that warm welcome I mentioned, we were invited to the afternoon's "Happy Hour" at 4pm. We immediately decided to go.

Now just stop right there.

This was not your normal "Happy Hour". It was strictly iced tea and coffee with a group of twenty or so retired folks simply living their lives together. After the "business" of the club, we visitors were invited to the front, handed a microphone and given an opportunity to make introductions. We were asked to tell a little bit about ourselves and why we chose the RV lifestyle... and SURPRISE! There it was. It was time to tell "the Story".

You see, for us, our Ministry plan and mission statement is to "tell our story anywhere, anytime". I assumed that meant personally and in churches, but when I least expected it, I was handed an unexpected opportunity. I'm going to guess that this "Happy Hour" was not quite what they were used to.

That evening we gave away two books. For those of you not acquainted with our Ministry Plan, you might miss the significance of this. You see, we have committed to give a copy of TEARS IN A BOTTLE free of charge to every parent we come across who has also lost a child.

The following day we enjoyed a day trip to Cloudcroft New Mexico. This immediately called for a visit to a thrift store for a second hand sweatshirt (we weren't prepared for the difference in temperature at 9000 feet in the early spring).

We discovered an incredible location for lunch high in the New Mexico Mountains overlooking White Sands National Monument. The renovated 1906 lodge and restaurant wouldn't take my Chili's gift card, so someone reading this bought our lunch. Thank you, and don't worry. We're still frugal! Tip included, it was less than $20!

An amazing mountain drive through New Mexico back roads completed a magical day. Back at "The Ranch" later that evening (now that sentence sounds like part of a good old western movie), I removed our bicycles  for the first time from their home on the bike rack, aired the tires and then took a spin around this quaint RV subdivision.

Everyone was more than friendly and the experience was a veritable education on fulltime RVing. As we rounded the last corner I spotted a gentlemen who we met at "Happy Hour" the previous day. He was sitting in his lawn chair in front of his Holiday Rambler motorhome. I rode into his driveway and immediately noticed that he was sitting in the shade reading a book... SURPRISE!

A few moments later when he tried to tell me what my book meant to him, he began to cry. You see, this is one of the books we had just given away. He also shares our Journey.

As we enter this phase of the two-year odyssey, I am beginning to believe that the "Greater Journey" just might be waiting around every corner, even when I least expect it. I love to tell the story. For you see, Matt's story is my story. My story is Christ's story.

THE GREATER JOURNEY...

So here it comes. Every once in a while I have to say something to remind you that I really am a preacher. Ready?

When is the last time you told your story? It is not the same as mine, but if you know Christ, you have one. I don't have a corner on this whole "Greater Journey" thing. Make Christ's story real in your story and then share it with a world without hope.

I know that people often look like they have it "all together", but trust me, they don't. The world system is a mess. If you try to find happiness by finding happiness, you are doomed to defeat. You can only find lasting happiness by investing yourself in the happiness of others.

What better way is there to accomplish this than by telling your story of God's grace and leading them into a relationship with Christ?

CHAPTER 10
The Gift

What a gift this Journey has become for me.

After a few days in East Central New Mexico, including visits to two national and one state park, we headed north. Here a simple RVing lesson would make itself known: Not all pull through campsites are created equal.

We arrived at the Cochiti Lake Army Corp of Engineer's Recreation Park around four in the afternoon early that May. It's geographical location, situated on BLM land shared with the Cochiti Native people, is about halfway between Santa Fe and Albuquerque. This location assured that the drive was breathtaking to say the least.

Signage was minimal in the park, but thanks to some "good Samaritans" in a pickup truck we found where to check in. I reserved this RV site online, sight unseen. You cannot imagine how relieved I was when the park attendant offered his congratulations, stating that I had reserved the most beautiful site in the park.

We wound through on new concrete roads to the very back of the camping loop where we found site 58. It was of reasonable size, and the nearly 90 degree turn at the front made it very easy to pull through, if you own a trailer about half the size of ours that is. With a small dose of advice, a larger dose of stress and the addition of about 30 minutes, we had backed in the exit, set up and hooked up.

Only then I took a moment and honestly surveyed the scene. We were perched literally on a mountaintop surrounded on three sides by three different mountain ranges. The tallest of these were still capped by the winter's snow. Below was a beautiful man made lake created by interposing a giant earthen dam across the Rio Grande River.

The nearly new campsite itself was huge. It was all made of concrete, including a concrete pad and concrete picnic table covered by a beautiful brass colored roof. Even though surrounded by wide open high desert land, it had an unusual degree of privacy. For you "non campers", this is all a good thing!

The first sunrise the following morning assured me of the beautiful natural setting that would be our home base for the next several days. We were bookending our visit to this part of New Mexico with two Sunday opportunities to share the story...the foundation for this entire Journey.

My "work days" between those Sundays called for some brief audio and video production work, so I was on the hunt for the best location to set up. So how's this for "rethink remote recording studio"?

After balancing some fairly strenuous mountain hiking at the Tent Rocks National Monument with some more serious work, some newfound friends, a balloon ride (that I purchased well in advance when I still had a job) and some basic "touristy" days, it was time for our first opportunity to tell Matt's story in northeast New Mexico; and our first opportunity ever to worship with a Native American Church.

This first "opportunity" was an amazing of a Church service, better than most I have ever experienced. The small, warm, welcoming congregation gathered for coffee and fellowship earlier than most. After a relaxed teaching time they continued with

fellowship and a light breakfast. After nearly an hour of what someone in my career field might call "opening elements", it was our turn. We told our story and were blessed seeing its God driven impact on a different culture at a different Church in a different state. Following the service the congregants continued with fellowship and a full dinner. To say the least, these folks were in no hurry!

It was a tremendous lesson for us in how a different culture embraces worship, as well as a bit of a throwback to an earlier, perhaps an even better time. This was a glimpse into a time when Church was not something to be "figured into one's weekend" or merely scheduled for the hour before lunch. It was rather considered as a vital part of one's entire life. A time that counted relationship with God as the principle cornerstone of a holistic approach to community.

During dinner, I had the privilege to sit across from the Associate Pastor. He was a Navajo, and near my age. I asked him to talk to me about his life and his culture. About an hour later it was time to strike the stage and get on with the day; or more correctly, the evening. I left that conversation with two unique gifts in addition to making a new friend. I had an invitation to learn more and perhaps even accompany him on a future journey to the reservation to tell our story. Who knows what tomorrow's Journey holds, but I would treasure either gift.

The week between the Sundays was amazing as well. Tuesday brought a special visitor to us. Crested Butte, Colorado where Joe Jr., our oldest son is living was just over five hours away. He drove down to spend a few days with us. I viewed his arrival a bit differently than I would have before this Journey began. With our altered schedule at the first with the arrival of Keegan, I had already learned to watch for God in everything. What an awesome opportunity to bookend this first tour with yet another wonderful family opportunity.

Joe Jr., who has turned out to be quite a fine musician in his own right, makes his living doing the audio/video/lighting for a community organization in his hometown. For those of you reading this who know my family a little better, I'm talking about the same person we all know as "Joey". It seems that a few years, some advanced education; a marriage and a successful career can even alter a person's name. To everyone but Shaunda and me that is, we still call him "Joey".

I embraced hours of fishing, hiking and multiple trips to a particularly well-known discount department store chain (seems those poor folks in CB are three and one half hours from this "bastion of capitalism"). Add to that, three additional hours at a large music store and a few precious minutes of throwing a baseball. (Thanks son, for remembering the ball gloves… and especially the tradition it represents). Top it off with some great food courtesy of Shaunda and a trip up the Sandia Peak Tramway and you have one magical week.

The blessed common denominator in all of this activity for this father? The chance to just spend time with his son. I suppose it gave me another unexpected and almost surreal gift as well: to once again play pitch and catch with the little boy in front of the well scarred privacy fence that hid the propane tanks. The biggest difference? He throws too hard now. My hand hurt.

Thank you Lord for the gift of time. The precious gift you give us that once spent, can never be retrieved. Thank you for teaching me to "never take one moment for granted"… and for reminding me of that lesson learned as the baseball popped into the ball glove on that beautiful sunny spring afternoon in the New Mexico Mountains.

I believe that my son came to visit us for a few days so he could enjoy a much-deserved break. I remember the hard work it takes to build a family, and a life. I think he came to play a bit and to step away from all things musical and technical. But I would soon put him back to work.

The second of the "bookend Sundays" you see, would turn into a miraculous disaster.

THE GREATER JOURNEY...

Why do we allow time and schedules to dictate not only our life choices, but often our ability to find peace as well? Ever lie down in your bed at night, close your eyes and find yourself unable to simply "shut down"?

Here are some verses to read. Why not get someplace quiet or perhaps just shut the door and shut off your phone and let these verses speak to you?

Isaiah 40:31
Matthew 14:23
Mark 6:31
Ephesians 5:15-17
Matthew 11:28
1 Peter 5:7

Thought for the day...
What one practical change can I make today to ensure I will have one extra moment for God tomorrow? Do I view time as a "gift"?

CHAPTER 11
Miraculous Disaster

We arrived right on time for what is becoming our new "day before the event" routine: this time a Saturday setup. Meeting a day early gives us an opportunity to get acquainted with the Pastor as well as complete all the technical aspects before event day. Saturday setup came off without a hitch. This approach alleviates much of the stress of Sunday... in theory.

It was quite handy this time around to have a fresh set of muscles and tireless energy embodied in my son... my visitor, my gift. His past and current work experience made him way over qualified to help his Dad set audio and video (and even more importantly, carry the equipment in from the truck). I reminded Joe

Jr. that he was on vacation and didn't need to help at all. I am, however, quite grateful he refused to listen to me.

In addition to the extra muscles and needed energy, it was even more wonderful to have his intellect and experience as well... a thought process that comprehends the relative complexity of setting audio and video for a production like the LIVE WORSHIP EVENT.

With the audio and video setup complete, Joe Jr. tuned the room. He got it sounding pretty good. The only thing left to do was to switch everything off and head out for the day. The next morning we returned to the same room for a brief, final level and equipment check. Everything fired right up, including the video, and we were ready to go. We changed locations in the church plant for Sunday School, so we once again switched off the hand me down projector to conserve bulb life.

Enter the disaster...

Ready to start the service, a few minutes later we entered the Sanctuary. I reached down and switched the projector back on. This time I was met with the flashing red light of death (indicating lamp failure) and the corresponding dark screen.

"No problem", I said, perhaps even out loud. After all, I had prepared for this scenario. I am a professional. I have spent my life in this "business". I have a spare bulb!

New and bigger problem; changing bulbs didn't help.

For those of you reading this who have not experienced the LIVE WORSHIP EVENT, this may not seem like that big of a deal. This service however, is something that falls outside the typical worship service description. I present the story through speaking, music and… video.

The use of video accomplishes a couple of important goals. It makes for a more compelling presentation as the addition of imagery supports the stories being told. Instead of just talking about Matt, I can show his picture as well as images of him leading worship. Instead of merely telling about him singing, I can also incorporate a few lines of actual audio. Hopefully, the video element keeps the worshipper engaged to a greater degree than would merely my speaking and music.

There is another benefit as well, although I rarely state it publicly. I use the videos to tell the parts of the story that are the most difficult for me to share while retaining some sense of decorum. The first of the three short videos tell of a personal failure to trust God earlier in my life. The second concerns Matt's death. The final tells the story of the day when hope first returned for Shaunda and me.

The service that morning began with ten minutes of the Worship Leader "treading water" while Joe Jr. and I attempted to conquer the projector failure. My visitor came to the rescue. His brief break from this type of work now indisputably over, Joe Jr. performed every possible electronic lifesaving technique, yet the aging projector refused to cooperate. A restart however, got us moving in the right direction and I began the event.

Midway through the first video, the process had to be repeated.... Midway through the second video it had to be repeated yet again. Through the music portions in between it was repeated a time or two more.

The worshippers in attendance that morning were engaged, supportive, tearful and visibly moved... but I feared they would soon become as distracted as I was.

Yet another restart, and the final video began. I was sitting on the front pew when the Pastor's wife leaned in beside me and whispered in my ear. "This kind of thing happens all the time. Don't worry about it, we're all praying for you and we've got your back."

Midway through that final video, we blackscreened for a final time. I wasn't sure what to do, but almost instinctively I stepped to the keyboard and picked up the narrative of the video midstream and supported it with a quiet piano music bed. I told the remainder of the story live, tears and all, and then segued into the final song. Just keys and vocal this time; no backing tracks… or video.

The unexpected benefit here was that Joe Jr. and Shaunda (my "Technical Director") were now entirely unplugged from the event. They could simply relax and join their fellow worshippers.

Here's a recap… After the 10 minutes of treading water, the LIVE WORSHIP EVENT had now been condensed into well under forty minutes; most of the first thirty thoroughly wrought with disaster. The last ten had been presented in a vastly different, much shortened format without the familiar technological support.

I finished the story and took my seat feeling a great deal more than marginally embarrassed. I began to rationalize this event as a "lesson learned" and was already making plans for a much needed trip to purchase a new projector.

The LIVE WORSHIP EVENT presents three themes. The message of unbelievable hope in Christ, the question "Can God Be Trusted?" and the challenge to "Never take one moment of life for granted".

I share the reality of a powerful Savior who champions the lost cause and introduces hope into life's most hopeless situations.

I tell of a personal Savior who never leaves us in spite of our failure, and can without question always be trusted.

I then encourage a response of like kind by urging a commitment to make the most of every moment we have. I also ask the worshippers to take whatever practical steps needed to facilitate the healing of broken relationships.

As I was sinking deeper into the front pew that morning, I was really just waiting; waiting for the closing elements to grant me release from my prison of failure. I was really hoping someone had already started the truck!

The Pastor's wife, who was handling the platform duties, stepped to the microphone and simply said: "I think we need to have an invitation". An "invitation" for those of you who may be unfamiliar, is the opportunity given in a worship service to respond publicly to a movement of God experienced privately.

As this opportunity to respond began, I slipped back to the keyboard and began quietly playing an old hymn...

> *Softly and tenderly, Jesus is calling.*
> *Calling for you and for me*

Enter the miraculous...
It seems that ten minutes of "treading water" and forty minutes of a more than slightly unhinged LIVE WORSHIP EVENT was destined to be followed by thirty minutes of response... and a moving of the Holy Spirit like I have experienced on far too few occasions.

> *Come home, Come home*
> *Ye who are weary, come home.*

I will not go into detail about what else happened… or more accurately I cannot go into more detail. During those thirty minutes God was moving in the places in people's hearts that no one except the individual himself can see. Let's just say this:

A grandson accepted Christ…
A prodigal son came home…
Lives were changed…
People embraced hope…

All present that day shared in the glory. After the service the same Spirit continued. Both Shaunda and I spent time with multiple people who were moved by the events of that miraculous morning movement of the Spirit of God..

The last person who spoke with me (before we finally got around to striking the stage) was a man about my age. He was quite well dressed and had taught our morning Bible Study. Before speaking he removed from his Bible a well worn folded sheet of standard letter sized paper and handed it to me. There was a photo of a young man on the top half. I recognized it immediately as what us "churchy folks" would refer to as a program or a bulletin.

Fighting through his now freely flowing tears, he began to speak.

"This", he said, "is my son".

The handout was from his son's memorial service, not yet two years in the past. His son's picture was on the front.

In retrospect, I guess I might be off on my timing a bit… it could be that "The Miraculous" had entered long before I sensed it was there. Perhaps it was my preoccupation with the "lesser things" that kept me from recognizing its entrance.

One of the lessons from TEARS IN A BOTLE, Lessons From A Broken Heart is that my life is not all about me; it is rather, all about God. The Almighty One certainly isn't in the least dependent on backing tracks, videos, music, slick productions, technology, marketing, oratory… or me for that matter.

It is an absolute fact that all of those things pale in comparison to the value of the presence and power of the Holy Spirit moving in the hearts of people.

OK… here comes a terrifying prayer for someone like me who is often far too obsessed with "perfection in the presentation". I'd like you to pray this with me as well:

"God, please bring the miraculous, even if it requires that disaster accompany it."

Hmmm…. Am I still talking about our worship, or am I now speaking of our lives?

Perhaps both.

Perhaps they are really supposed to be the same thing.

THE GREATER JOURNEY...

I like to be in control. There, I said it. I like to plan things out and then watch things go exactly the way I planned them. Seems though, that living by faith may have something to do with realizing that no matter how much I think I am in control of everything, I am really in control of nothing.

Consider these questions...
What does it mean to "trust God"?

Why do you think it is so hard for us to simply trust God?

Can God really take the "messes" of your life and turn them into something better?

Read *(and consider memorizing)* **Proverbs 3:5,6**

CHAPTER 12
Chasing Spring

I was raised in Northeastern Ohio where we had four distinct seasons of relatively equal length. Beginning with "Decoration Day" (Memorial Day), summers were warm and humid. This meant long hours of seasonal work for my Father; and long days of outdoor adventure for me. Summer also included our yearly family vacation.

Labor day weekend ushered in autumn with its colorful leaves that assured a small boy that mandatory Sunday afternoon drives would soon be underway. These weekend excursions were a welcome respite from the weekday routine of school... now officially underway.

Winter was fairly predictable as well. Our geographical location placed us in close proximity to the Canadian border and Lake Erie. This guaranteed a touch of lake effect snow mixed in with the standard snowfall. That snow would make its appearance as beautiful white flakes falling to earth bringing with it coats, gloves, hats, scarves... and sleds! Cold temperatures combined with those winter snows and long nights all but guaranteed small mountains of dark, dirty residue would remain all around my neighborhood long after the snow quit falling.

And then there was spring. Spring was a time of new beginnings when the slowly warming temperatures would take its daily toll on those "dark, dirty mountains" until they disappeared completely. The moisture left behind by the melting snow combined with the sunshine to produce a vibrant green in the surrounding yards and fields. Those same fields would soon be decorated by hundreds of yellow dandelions. Trees would bud and returning birds would sing... and the transition to a season of new life would soon be complete.

I have always loved spring. It was a refreshing season of hope when a small boy's dreams could touch the sky; dreams of summer little league, "sleeping in", glorious adventures to the beach or the mountains and baseball in the middle of the street until dark. Why sometimes I was even allowed to stay outside until the streetlights came on.

On our trip from Tyler to Fort Davis Shaunda and I marveled how the West Texas trees were already budded out and the grass turning green. The fast track return trip to Tyler was almost like turning back the calendar. We returned to a place not yet touched by the same climatic conditions. That cycle was destined to repeat itself. To New Mexico, around New Mexico and back, we experienced spring over and over. What an unexpected blessing to find ourselves "Chasing Spring".

Here I sit on the morning of "Decoration Day"; what we now call Memorial Day. Three years of planning for this great adventure, and three months of living in the preparation for that great adventure has been overwhelming to say the least.

Yesterday was Sunday, and we didn't have a Church scheduled. We spent the preceding week in Branson Missouri accompanied by Makenna, our precious granddaughter. It will likely be well past summer before we once again tow "the Virge" down familiar Texas highways.

This past week was comprised of exactly what you might expect from such a diverse trio of travelers: walks, a pet show, a trip to a zoo, a ride on the "ducks", fast food (from chain restaurants offering kid's meals that come with a toy), fishing (with an eight year old) and the like... You get the picture. Nothing that adults would ever choose to do, but everything grandparents love to do.

Without a place to tell our story on this Memorial Day weekend, we visited a familiar Church in Eureka Springs. The Pastor is a long-time and dear friend... a man for whom I have long held great respect. Before we ever began this Journey, I asked four churches to partner with us. We told our story to their congregations and asked them to genuinely pray for us. This was one of those Churches.

I truly enjoyed their unique presentation of Missions and I played one song on the piano to close the service. After the service, I was standing at the back shaking hands and thanking people for their prayers. A couple, several years younger than us, approached and introduced themselves. With the rainy weather finally predicted to give way to a day of sunshine, they had made a last minute trip to this beautiful area to play golf.

As the gentlemen shook my hand he said: "the Pastor says I need to read your book".

"Why did he say that?" I asked.

The answer? They had lost their adult son just two months earlier.

If you know Christ and if you now understand the spirit of what we are doing, I don't have to write any more. You already know what happened over the next few moments.

They came to play golf. We came to say thank you. God had other plans for all of us.

Do you see coincidence? I think not. I see miraculous.

We made the hour long drive through the breathtaking Ozark mountain countryside back to the tiny RV park. We loaded back on "The Virge". (Come on… wait for it… you remember what "The Virge" is). Shaunda and I soon stepped outside to occupy the lawn chairs for a few minutes while Makenna ran back and forth in the RV. She was talking out loud and playing "babysitter", with her pink bear and new stuffed brown dog in tow. After a few minutes I no longer heard the patter of tiny feet… so I knew it was time to see what was going on.

I found her curled up in our bed with the covers pulled up to her chin... next to that tiny brown dog. She had a rather perplexed look on her face.

"What are you doing?" I asked.

"I was wondering" she replied, "Would you help me with the words to ask Jesus in my heart?"

Did you see that coming? I didn't, yet I somehow wasn't really all that surprised either.

Once again the miraculous burst to the forefront. Once again if you know Christ and if you now understand the spirit of what we are doing, I don't have to write any more. You already know what happened over the next few moments.

Sometimes, like last night, when I lie down and close my eyes, there just aren't nearly enough words to thank God for his immeasurable grace... and the life sustaining hope we have in Christ.

You see, for us, much of the harshness of this particular season of winter is now becoming more of a distant memory. The warmth of God's grace expressed in the miraculous is ever present these days; melting the final vestiges of this particular darkness from our daily consciousness. In it's place remain the beautiful memories of Matt... and his life well lived.

I do understand this reality however, and I pray that you do as well. Seasons have a funny way of repeating themselves. We must always remember to worship during the cold chill of winter and its accompanying bleakness, as well as the bright, warm, life renewing sunshine of spring.

We have literally chased spring through the mountains of four states and found it living around us daily in the miraculous. Now that our first tour, "Chasing Spring", is in the history books. We head "North of the Red River" in two days... and for the entirety of the summer.

Time for me to get up from the computer now. Seems that early morning has given way to late morning and my eight year old beautician is done with my hairstyle and manicure... and is desiring further "interaction"... and I don't want to miss a moment.

I guess I'll just close the first part of our "Journey of a Lifetime" with this reminder: Yes Shaunda, everything still is about music... at least to me. So here is yet one more song reference, this one from my high school days. It seems rather apropos here... Ready for it? Here it comes:

"We've Only Just Begun".

Part 3
North of the Red River

CHAPTER 13
Then Again...

I've always heard that once you leave a place, you can't ever go home again. I was never quite sure where that thought came from until I ran across an old book by a similar title. "You Can't Go Home Again" is a novel written by a man named Thomas Wolfe. It was published after his death in 1940. The narrative tells the story of a fictional character named George Webber, himself a young author, who writes a book that refers to his hometown of Libya Hill.

The story line goes that George Webber has already written a very successful novel about his family and his hometown. Upon returning to that town, rather than finding that warm welcome he desires, he discovers that he is considered more of a traitor/tyrant than a hometown hero. Seems the town didn't appreciate him telling quite so much about them.

The fictional author finally reaches the conclusion that "You can't go back home to your family... You can't go back home to your childhood... You can't go back home to your dreams... You can't go back home to the "escapes of Time and Memory." It's just that "you can't go home again".

Our first stop to tell the story "North of the Red River" was in Akron, Ohio; my hometown. I lived in Akron until I was 22, and in that general area for several years after that. My next church was only a few miles down the road. Needless to say, being back home was an especially emotionally charged experience for me.

Being home again demanded a trip through the community where I spent my formative years. On one side of the street was the house where I first took piano lessons. Around the corner next to my house was the Church I attended as a child, and where I came to know Christ. The church's parking lot was where we used to park our big red and silver bus. It was also where I used to do "donuts" after an evening out with my buddies. My dad watched over that church like a hawk. We would always take a couple trips around the block so he wouldn't connect the dots. You know how long it took me to tell my Dad it was my friends and me all along? It was years later and he still didn't laugh.

On the corner in that small "subdivision of the sixties" stood my childhood home. My family moved there when I was just four years of age. It's a good thing I remembered the address. Can you believe someone put a different color siding on the house? And built a deck on the front? And put up a fence? And cut down the live Christmas Tree my dad and I planted in the front yard after the Holidays? And built a garage? And of all things…tore down my basketball goal?

What's wrong with people? It was fine the way it was. Seems like they could have just left it alone. It's only been forty years.

Wow. Maybe you can't go back home.

Then Shaunda and I continued our drive down nostalgia lane. There was my Elementary school...or rather where it used to be. Someone tore it down. There's my Junior High, except for the fact that its been entirely remodled and/or replaced. It just didn't look "right". Next, let's check out the bowling alley where I spent so many Saturday mornings. Nope, completely gone.

The Church where I first served as a vocational minister? Years ago it combined with another church across town. Is there nothing that is truly stable? Anything that was the same yesterday; and is still the same today?

In Psalm 73 David was struggling with the prosperity of the wicked. He was wondering why bad people go on through life seemingly untouched by the justice they deserve. While my struggle is not in that same area, the solution he discovered was the same one I would now utilize, and to great effect.

"Then I went into the house of God..." David said.   For me, it was time for church, time to tell the story. Inside that wonderful, safe place of fellowship I found many old friends (literally, *old* friends). But that was ok, I was older as well. I also made many new friends.

I left Family Fellowship a few months ago after a thirty-five year ministry career, the last twenty-one right there in Greenville Texas. I felt like I had enjoyed a fair bit of longevity. In this particular Church in Ohio where I was now to present Matt's story, is found one of my dearest lifelong friends. This is a friend I knew from Elementary School (the one that used to be there) through High School. We then continued on and graduated from the same Bible College together and worked on same Church staff together. Unbelieveaby, he is still in his original place of service, forty plus years later, now as Senior Pastor; talk about longevity. I'm not even in the running.

I also enjoyed a wonderful conversation with his adult daughter, whom I remember as being a little girl. I stood in amazement as she told me how her daughter (who she remembers as being a little girl) had recently graduated from high school. Where do the years go?

My former Pastor was there as well. Now well into retirement, he was the first Pastor I ever called "boss", and still the only place I ever worked that I was required to show up for work with a Bible *and* a racquetball racquet. He is still one of the greatest public speakers I have ever heard. And now I had to speak publicly with him in the congreagation.

Then there were the others. There were the men who modeled for me what it meant to be a Christian husband long before I was afforded either opportunity. These were my heroes from yesterday. This one man in particular defined for me what someone my age should look like as a genuine Christian father. I had the privilege of sitting down and having supper with him and his wife. This time I would watch him model what being a genuine Christian Grandfather looked like.

Then there were the men I have known since before any of us were men. We were barely teenage boys when we piled on that big diesel bus and travelled all across the country in search of our future. We all agreed that we left most of our musical dreams somewhere out on the highway, but we all kept a lifetime of amazing memories.

There were faces in the congregation of those who taught me how to be a Pastor and loved me anyway when I was proven a slow learner. There were also reminders in nearly every conversation of those whose faces can no longer be seen with physical eyes.

I remember a staff Pastor that served at this Church long before either the now Senior Pastor or I were even out of Junior High School. He joined the staff of this great Church in 1969. As I shared an embrace with him after all these years I learned that he was still serving on the staff of this Church... at ninety-four years of age.

And then the telling of the story began that day. Once again the Spirit of God moved in ways that I have no words to adequately describe. Perhaps, multiplied by the faces in the congregation and the memories they represented, the experience was personally moving.

It may have also been even more poignant because of this truth: In my opening comments of THE GREATER JOURNEY Live Worship Event I share a story of Matt's first experience with music. I tell of a guitar I gave him on that day when he learned his first three chords. I also tell how I went to my closet and retrieved that old dusty guitar I had been given years earlier. On this day, halfway back in the center section sat the lady who had given me that same guitar at least thirty-five years earlier.

Then again, it could have been the elderly gentleman who clutched two bent photographs through the entirety of the service. When I sat on the front pew near Shaunda while the first video played, he leaned up from his pew and showed them to me. The first was a family picture and the other a much older photo of one of the people in the first photo. This time though, that person was a small girl seemingly frozen in time. He told me that this was his treasure. He got a free book.

As the story went on that morning, it was funny how the faces of some in the congregation were the exact same faces that appeared in the video that covers my early years. We looked a bit different though for some strange reason.

We all shed some tears on this day. However, after much reflection, I believe I have determined what seemed so different during this presentation of the story; what was so moving to me. I believe it was the way the congregation worshipped during the corporate worship opportunities in the Live Worship Event. I'm not sure I have ever heard voices that sang so strong and so confident combined with so many lifted hands and so many tear filled faces. It was glorious.

After the service was complete, Shaunda found herself once again with her arms around yet another mother who shared a similar Journey... and giving away yet another book. I stepped to the lobby. The mood around the table that held my books was an indescribable melting pot of joy, tears, hugs, memories and stories... so many stories.

When the crowd thinned out after several memorable moments, that ninety-four year old staff Pastor came by once again; this time to say goodbye; I mean "so long". Although I have known this servant of God for many years, I somehow missed that he had his own story too. I listened as he shared it with me through free flowing tears. I gave away one more book.

The next day, bolstered by a weekend of even more unforgettable experiences, Shaunda and I drove back to the area of town where I was raised so we could take a walk. The walk was in a huge grassy area covering literally dozens and dozens of acres. It was bedecked with thousands of granite markers placed there over many decades. Armed with a map and after a few moments of searching, I literally stumbled on two markers that bore the same last name as mine; and the first names of my parents.

After a few moments of silence with Shaunda holding my right hand in both of hers, we began to walk back towards our truck. As we slowly walked, the last verse of a familiar hymn rang in my head as if a choir were singing.

> *Time is now fleeting, the moments are passing.*
> *Passing from you and from me.*
> *Shadows are gathering, Deathbeds are coming.*
> *Coming for you and for me.*

In my imagination I could see families standing by every graveside. Some were dressed in tie-dye and ripped jeans, both girls and boys with long flowing hair. Others were attired in centuries old settler's garb while still others were in finely pressed military uniforms.

Other groups consisted of men who wore a suit and tie, with slicked back hair and thick black rimmed glasses. The women accompanying them wore conservative longer skirts and had their hair twisted on the tops of their heads. All were surrounded by their familes.

You see, this is the place where all stand on equal ground, and all are found wanting in the presence of a Holy God. Remember what David said in Psalm 73? After he factored God into the equation, he understood their end. And that helps me understand mine as well.

One day we will all stand before God. We will not be questioned about our giving record, our political views nor our family pedigree. Only one question will beg an answer at that moment... the most important moment of all eternity for us:

"What have you done with Jesus?"

For you see, if we know Christ, there are many things worse than death. If we do not know Christ, there is nothing worse than death. Death is merely a doorway; a doorway to eternity. Simply stated, Jesus Christ *is* that one "thing" that is the same yesterday, today and forever. And He still says that if you plan to come to God, you must come by way of Him. No "plan B". No bartering. Simply the eternal "must". You "must" come by the way of the cross. You "must" be born again.
It is the sacrifice of Christ on the cross and the great hope that we find in Him that makes it possible for me to tell our story. It is that same hope that allows believers to raise their hands and confidently worship in spite of their tears; and the very same hope that

empowers a ninety-four year old man to serve faithfully in the ministry for the majority of those years, in spite of his painful loss.

Lord, I truly don't know what the future holds, or what awaits us past this two year "Journey of a Lifetime", but I find myself once again overwhelmed by your grace. I also find myself thoroughly humbled that you would allow me to tell this story publicly; and then bless it with Your indescribable presence.

We closed that first service "North Of The Red River" by singing together the chorus of that same hymn I heard in my heart the following day at the cemetery:

Come Home, Come Home.
Ye who are weary come home.
Earnestly, Tenderly Jesus is calling.
Calling, Oh sinner, Come home.

So it has been said that you really can't ever go home. Then again, maybe you can.

THE GREATER JOURNEY...

I am keenly aware that not everyone has great memories of their childhood or their childhood homes. Some of you may have read my words and found the emotions linked with them strangely missing.

You may have experienced rejection at home, physical abuse, mental abuse or worse. I have learned that sometimes God pictured as a "Father" is a bit of a turn off to some. They know primarily their earthly fathers and have known violence, aloofness or complete abandonment. Home may have held nothing but pain for you.

Please stop for a moment and imagine what the "ideal" father might be. Loving, kind, firm, tender, understanding, fair. Then regardless of your upbringing, why not consider the verse at the bottom, and then consider taking a few moments right now to thank God for this unbelievable gift.

Remember, regardless of where you have been, your Heavenly Father stretches His arms out to welcome you "Home". You can go home again.

Psalm 68:4-6

CHAPTER 14
SAAAAAAALUUUUUUTE!
Part 1

Bear Branch Indiana.
Population 17
SAAAAAALUUUUTE!

No; seriously... Population 17.

For those of you who don't understand the 70's TV reference, head to your favorite video site and search "HEE HAW".

After a quick trip to the East Coast accompanied by dear friends to celebrate a personal milestone by dipping our toes in the Atlantic Ocean, we headed west to Indiana. But not before another wonderful weekend experience in Ohio. We interacted with old friends and made new friends, and we especially enjoyed another awesome moving of the Spirit of God. There were more amazing stories from this day, one of which you will read about in a future chapter.

Did I ever tell you about the guy I knew in High School that had the really cool car? I just realized that the opening sentence of this paragraph appears a bit random, if not more like the opening line of a bad joke begging a witty one liner. I assure you it is neither.

I was in my teens, somewhere in the early 70's, and I had already formed my first music group. My bass player called and asked if I was at home. He said he had something to show me. About thirty minutes later the ground began to shake as he roared down the street in his latest treasure... a 1967 bright red Dodge Charger. Yeah, that one. The one with the 440 PI (police interceptor) engine. The one with too many carburetors each having too many barrels.

And then the magic... he tossed me the keys.

I will not divulge exactly what happened next for fear my children, scratch that, I mean for fear my grandchildren may read this one day and want to give it a try. I will only say that it started with "Go ahead, jump on it" and it ended about a quarter of a mile down the public roadway with my world turned around... literally. I had completed a 180 degree turn and was now looking the wrong way down the street. Oh yeah, I was screaming as I recall. Screams that you could not understand unless you have piloted (I use that word intentionally) a genuine muscle car.

As the service was about to begin that morning, that same friend walked in the door. I smiled; we shared a bear hug. Amazingly, we both looked exactly like we did on that crazy summer day more than forty years earlier. Well, maybe not. I guess the miles had changed us both quite a bit. This time, instead of trading dreams of future stardom, we instead set about sharing pictures of our Grandchildren. Not a bad tradeoff either, I might add.

As I started towards the front of the church to begin that morning's "telling of the story", he reached in his pocket and held up a set of antiquated car keys. No chip in these keys. No keyless entry. No kidding.

"She's out there," he said. "Maybe after service you'd like to take her for another spin."

My first thought was to crank up the tempos, cut three songs or simply begin with something like: "We're glad you're here, I hope today is a blessing, you are dismissed". Thankfully though, I regained my perspective, eased back and let God do what only He can do. You see, God is not all that impressed with my piano playing, my speaking ability or my wit (Shaunda would question if the last two even exist at all, and I fear she may be right). It is amazing though, what can happen in a public worship service when He is truly at the center. Actually, I mostly just watch these days... watch in amazement at what God can do with the little I have to offer.

After the service that morning I spoke with several more Journeyers who had shared a similar road. We swapped stories, tears and hugs; and I gave away even more books. I spoke with the Pastor, that same man who had been at this same Church when I left Ohio in the 1980's. Here was yet another true, quiet hero who has been about the business of the Kingdom with a lifetime commitment to a group of people. I met the person considered his successor. A young man full of ideas and energy yet committed to learning and humility. I saw in him a continued promise of a bright future for this great Church.

Then came the striking of the stage and the loading of the truck... and finally that old familiar magic came calling as my friend once again tossed me his keys. The keys to a 1967 red Charger...but not any red charger... the same red Charger. He had never sold her, nor restored her, nor did anything to her except show her the love and meticulous care she deserved. To be quite honest, unlike my friend and I, she really hadn't changed one bit. She honestly did look exactly the same.

"Two pumps of the accelerator and she'll start right up" came his instruction. No modern frills here, just good old-fashioned muscle car "technology". Shortly after following his instructions to the letter, the ground underneath me once again began to shake.

And so I dropped her in drive...
    And I took my foot off the brake...
        And...

I mostly let her coast all the way across the parking lot. This time I was at least a bit more mature. I understood the power that beckoned my right foot. I realized the responsibility entrusted me. I understood her value as well. I don't have any idea what my friend paid for this car in the 70's, but I am quite certain it would sell for ten times that now, or more. Look it up. There were only a few hundred of these ever built, and this one is an immaculate survivor.

And so I treated her with the respect she deserved, even though it was killing me.

Have you ever stopped and wondered how you are still alive? I know that I do. I don't know for certain, maybe it has to do with the losses we experience in this life. Perhaps it has something to do with going back to your hometown and reliving many of the things you did, even some of the dumb things.

Things like "Cadillac Hill". That's the place where if you give it the gas at just the right time you are destined to leave the ground at the first dip only to land on the steepest grade of the hill. It is there that you floor it. The final maneuver is to try and gauge where to "lock 'em up" to avoid sliding into the steady traffic at the main road at the bottom of the hill. Perfecting this type of thing takes a lot of practice. Funny though, when you recall that completing this feat in another buddy's 1966 fastback Mustang after having "thrown back a few brewskies", seemed to make perfectly good sense. Today I find myself in a strange state of embarrassment at being so foolish and grateful to have lived through it. It's just that we were young and it seemed ok to "jump on" life and "go for it" with little thought of consequence.

We then turn around a couple times, make a few bad choices, endure some near misses and it all looks so different. Now I understand so much more the frailty of life, and the amazing grace of God. Grace that allows us to breathe one more breath, to see one more sunrise, to take one more walk on the beach at sunset; toes in the water, shoes in one hand, each other's hand in the remaining. And you once again recognize that life is precious.

Father, teach me again today the lesson from yesterday; The lesson we must learn again every day. Your lesson that I share with hurting people every week. Even when heartache tries to strangle the life out of your dreams, there is hope. Our God can be trusted, even when life doesn't make sense. And that we must make the choice to "Never take one moment of life for granted" and choose to worship in the darkness.

You see, I hadn't missed a thing by not acting like a child again by doing more donuts on the Church parking lot. With today's perspective, coasting across the parking lot with the thunder under my feet was every bit as exciting as "turning her around in the road". I was merely choosing to respect her, and not mistreat her.

I shifted the lever back to "P" and reluctantly switched off the thunderous powerplant. When I stepped out, Shaunda was standing right there; grinning from ear to ear!

"Well?" she asked? Do you feel like you're sixteen again?"

I never answered her.

I just grinned right back.

THE GREATER JOURNEY…

Read…
Acts 11:22,23

Consider…
What does the grace of God mean to you? Can you look to a time in life when God miraculously spared you? Did you ever wonder why? Did you deserve such an intervention in your life?

Why not take a moment and thank God for His amazing grace. Why not launch a private time of worship with a few strains of Amazing grace, how sweet the sound. That saved a wretch like me". Better yet, why not do both?

I might suggest that to genuinely worship God for who He is requires us to see ourselves for who we are.

CHAPTER 15
SAAAAAAALUUUUUUTE!
Part 2

Back to Bear Branch Indiana.
Population 17
SAAAAAAALUUUUTE!

As a part of their programming, the 70's country music TV show HEE HAW would extend a "tongue in cheek" recognition to some random small town in America by giving the town name, population and then declare a long drawn out "SAAAAAALUUUUUTE!" In some way though, they were paying honor to "small town USA". In a similar spirit, this is my way of saluting; i.e. paying honor to a small town you've likely never heard of; Bear Branch, Indiana.

I'm not certain there has ever been a town selected for the pseudo honor of being the "Least Likely Place In America To Build A Great Church". If there were though, I would have no idea what town might be the winner, but I am quite confident that Bear Branch, Indiana would be a finalist.

Population 17? Yes, and that is no exaggeration. Bear Branch is a mere curve on a road that few travel, and certainly no common sense place to build a church. Still a small white frame building sits perched on a tight curve screaming to the uninformed passer by: "yesterday is alive and well". I have been in the ministry thirty-five years, and I can tell you that this is no place to build a church.

Here is the place where I get to tell Matt's story. We said "anytime, anywhere", and this particular stop was truly a gift from God and a gift from the Pastor who found a way to work us in. So I was genuinely grateful. My gratitude was accompanied however, by significantly lowered expectations. I believed that God would move in the services, and that lives would be touched. It's just that I figured the "lives touched" would likely be a handful of senior saints. At least I would still be in the minority when it comes to age.

Learning more about the Church upon our arrival, I was now fairly assured that my initial expectations would be fulfilled. The Pastor? He doesn't possess a Bible College education. The Worship Leader? Legally blind and partially deaf. No, I'm serious. The sanctuary? Pure, unadulterated 1940's complete with the Ten Commandments on the wall, a lithographed picture of "Long Haired Jesus" and the obligatory Attendance/Offering board. Buckle up boys, this ought to be quite a ride.

I was doing only a piano solo on Sunday morning as the Pastor had his service planned. I would tell our story on Sunday evening. Shaunda and I arrived at 9:45am for the 10am service, and we had our choice of seats. No prelude music. No countdown, no slick videos, no chance of a "real" church service. Do you sense another "Paul Harvey, Rest Of The Story" type of thing coming here? You probably should.

By service time, the small room was filled. Then the choir loft filled with families. Then the chairs came out. I looked around the room and found that I was correct. I was indeed in the minority considering age. This little country Church on the side of the highway in Bear Branch, Indiana Population 17, was jammed completely full of people... most under the age of 30.

The legally blind, partially deaf Worship Leader? All true.   She was also the Pastor's twenty three year old daughter who is a degreed musician majoring in Worship. She jumped up on the stage, guitar in hand (ok, hands!) and began to lead a familiar worship tune. This young lady without any challenges would have been considered a tremendous musician, and I don't say that lightly. I would have gladly welcomed her in any band I have ever led. With her challenges, she was borderline unbelievable.

And the people sang. And the people sang. And the people sang. No typo here with the repeated phrase. It was overwhelming. There were a handful of senior saints in attendance as well. They smiled and sang as well. Everyone even joined in and sang the Doxology. Seriously, and it was impressive, and moving. They didn't sing "Praise God from whom all blessings flow" lightly. I believe they meant it with the same conviction that characterizrd the Worship tunes. I immediately realized that I was indeed somewhere very special, and somewhere I really needed to be.

The tightly packed crowd only radiated the unseasonable early summer heat in southeastern Indiana. So much so that during the Worship the Pastor slipped to the windows, opened and then propped them up with a stick. "Don't worry" an older gentlemen whispered to me with a grin, "He's just adjusting the Thermostat". True story. Friends, it was hot. I mean HOT! And loud, did I say LOUD? There were children right in there with us. Yeah, in the Sanctuary with us! They screamed a bit, and cried a bit… and no one got overly concerned.

And the Pastor? No Bible College education. Notice I didn't say "no education". He is a brilliant yet humble man, bi-vocational by choice. He is the editor for two newspapers in neighboring communities and an extraordinary communicator and lover of people. He concluded the service with a profound, yet humble and challenging message concerning genuine love.

Later he privately told us about the "red envelopes". The "red envelopes" that their church distributes one to a family right before every Christmas. Each "red envelope" contains a crisp $100 bill. He told how their church people know that it is between them and God what to do with that money before Christmas. They are to carry it with them everywhere they go. If they do not find someone more in need than them, they are to keep it. If God brings them across someone in greater need, they are to give it away.

He told me of one church member who had her "red envelope" in her purse in the grocery checkout line. The lady in front of her with the children crawling all over presented a credit card as payment for the $99 and change grocery bill, only to have her card declined. The church member stepped up armed with her red envelope and said "I think I'm supposed to be behind you in line today".

How many life lessons are hidden here? How many sermons represented? Do you see why I say brilliant? Down in the trenches with his people, this is a Pastor who has discovered a truth often missed by many career ministers. Again I say, "Pastor" is not a position to be attained; it is rather a relationship to be earned.

I could tell you about the evening service and how once again God moved in incredible ways. I could mention the large number that returned, or the thirty plus teenagers on the wooden, unpadded front pews. Teenagers who stayed glued to Matt's story throughout the hour. I could elaborate on the powerful, strong worship at the conclusion with "Blessed Be Your Name", "You Never Let Go" and "How Great Is Our God". Did I mention that these people sang? I could tell you about the tears and the book I gave away...

Yet I feel it much more profitable to shine the light on this little church that shouldn't be, this oasis of the Spirit in the middle of nowhere. This group of people that have nurtured a heart for their community and their God.   Whether they needed me or not, I cannot say. I can assure you that I needed them.

In your mind, can you see that tiny white frame church on the sharp corner? Well look right behind and to the right and you will see the much larger building under construction. That same little church that had just sent seventy two teenagers to camp. Remember the "old time", familiar attendance and offering board? I won't give you the exact numbers. It might discourage those of us who have ministered in more populated areas. I will tell you this though, the difference between "enrollment" and "today's attendance"? Seven.

With yesterday honored, respected and included, open the doors to the small wooden structure and you will hear this place scream: "Tomorrow is alive and well". With the sound of their Worship still playing in my head, I pointed our truck north and west. I realized that there will likely always be a place in my memory for this white frame building on the sharp curve on that country road.

So let's face reality. You can't successfully blend the old and the new. People won't come if they're crowded. You've got to have air conditioning. Church members won't sit on hard pews.

You just can't build a church in rural America.

Hmmm..... Seems as if no one bothered to tell the folks in Bear Branch.

SAAAAAALUUUUUUUUTE!!!!!

THE GREATER JOURNEY...

This one may be too deep for a simple book like this. I feel confident that it is too deep for me. It is one simple question for you to ponder:

What makes a church a church?

CHAPTER 16
Stuck In A truck

"If you think I'm going to travel all across this country talking to you, you're nuts".

Perhaps a slightly less than loving statement when taken at face value. Undoubtedly well more than slightly humorous when considered in context.

Shaunda directed this statement of fact to me before we ever started down the highways and back roads of this beautiful nation. Shaunda has gone so far as to say that she thinks I may even have a "thinking disorder". She claims I analyze too much, dream too much and think too much. She also says I "talk too much". I'm not at all sure she is right, but I've been considering the validity of her statements and am spending many hours trying to determine if there is any truth contained therein along with determining any possible motivation. Oh wow, maybe she's right. I'll have to think about this some more.

One afternoon during the months of preparation for this "Journey of a Lifetime", Shaunda and I spent an afternoon together. As we drove down the Interstate towards a neighboring town that held a couple of shopping opportunities our hometown didn't, I was "waxing eloquent" (her words) about one of the deeper truths of life, or perhaps something fairly shallow for that matter. It was at that point that she blurted out that blatantly unkind comment.

"If you think I'm going to travel all across this country talking to you, you're nuts".

We then laughed for a long time together as we talked and considered the adventure to come. Then it became quiet. Then two seconds passed. Then I started talking again. Then we went in a store and purchased coordinating t-shirts.

Her's says, "Do Me A Favor and Stop Talking". Mine says, "I'm not arguing, I'm explaining why I'm right". True story... there's even a picture.

When we first planned for this crazy thing we're now in the middle of, one of the greatest concerns Shaunda verbalized was the fear of finding herself thousands of miles from home enveloped by a social void. Better stated, she had a fear of being stuck in a truck with me, all day, everyday!

I can't say that I blame her, considering we were leaving friends and family behind and facing more than a bit of uncertainty ahead. I assured her that God would indeed meet that need. I told her that God might send people our way who would fill that void. To be quite honest, I wasn't certain how any of this would happen. I was certain though, that God would meet her need and to that end I prayed.

So toward the Journey we ran. It was about time too. I had lots to say.

Almost immediately God brought people across our path. People with names like Bob, Anthony, Cassie, Dean, Bruce, Bernard, Russell, Elaine, Mary, Bert and Ernie (sorry, couldn't resist) and so many others. We would come into a different area of this country and begin conversations with titles like "Pastor, Mr. or Mrs.". Within days or weeks those introductory descriptive words would be lost, and somehow these folks simply become known as "friend".

It's hard to describe to someone who is not a Christ follower what happens inside the relationships of those who are. It may be equally impossible for that person to truly comprehend. Let me try and explain, at least from my perspective

Through my life I have known men who are hunters. I have known others who are athletes or fishermen. I have known yet others who are so passionate about the latter that they would claim they should be considered the former. I know a gentleman who creates beautiful wood cabinetry, another who paints breathtaking pictures, and still another who designs amazing machines for our nation's defense. There are those who play pool while others swim in theirs. There are gamers, bowlers and rock climbers. I have buddies who ride bikes: mountain, road and motor. I have others who physically cannot get up from the chair they are seated in without assistance.

I do not hunt. I do not fish (unless I'm with my children or grandchildren, where I'm the expert). I am assured to be the last one chosen in a game of pick-up basketball. I can't join two pieces of wood successfully nor can I complete even a somewhat aesthetically pleasing paint by number. I cannot make anything mechanical function even when armed with the instructions. I've never attacked a rock face and my game console of choice is still a PS3. "Scratch" is what I do behind my left ear and my only attempt at motorcycling involved a scooter.

Yet I would call every one of these men friend, son or fellow journeyer. I could pick up the phone and call any of them right now if I found myself in need. Yet on the outside we seem to have little in common.

Please stay with me here. I may be doing that "talking all the time thing" again, this time with my buddy Mac. At least Shaunda gets a break. Wait a minute… is that why the last thing she said this morning before going out the door to watch a Pastor's children during a church funeral was "why don't you blog this morning"? Never mind. Let's go on.

I love to make music. I enjoy being a Pastor. I have been blessed with a wonderful parallel career in law enforcement. I enjoy writing. Give me a set of headphones, a good vocal recording microphone, a keyboard, audio interface, and my computer, and I won't bother anyone for days.

I have family, friends and fellow Journeyers that love all these things as well. "That's easy to understand" you might say. You have much in common with them. Yet there are many musicians with whom I do not share common goals, and some Pastors as well for that matter. There are cops I know extremely well, yet we are not close to at all.

So what is the unifying factor? What makes us as Christ followers relationally close to some who are unlike us and distant from others who are? It is the same supernatural Force that makes strangers become friends, and yet can turn friends into strangers.

Seems that in this world, and unfortunately in some churches as well, many have once again missed the unifying factor of simply being a genuine disciple of Christ. We may have, once again, in an unending search to make Christ fit in with us, erred in not realizing that it is us that need to fit in with Christ.

In my lifetime I have watched organized religion in what was initially an attempt to genuinely please God, institute a set of rules to assure spiritual compliance. Many of these rules found their origin in excellent Biblical "non debatables" if you will. The rule list then was supplemented by conclusions based on "Biblical principles". All too soon however, the rule list also became polluted with self-determined, often geographical or socially inspired addendums. The end result of this type of degradation of purpose was the minimization of the personal discipleship experience and the convicting work of the Holy Spirit altogether. It was replaced by the list. Intentionally or not, Christianity became about the rules, not about the Savior.

Not to be outdone, many of us young Christians from the 60's and 70's joined in with society's then overt "revolution" mentality. Like those around us, we questioned all forms of governmental, religious and personal authority. Many of us found ourselves in the spiritual world challenging the whole "rule thing"; rejecting it as "outward Christianity". We embraced an "inward Christianity", and I believe rightly so, as a more pure form of Christian living. Simply stated, our good works don't make us a Christian. Our relationship with Christ produces good works.

And the pendulum began to swing.

Fast-forward to today's brand of Christianity. We live in a world system further and further removed from morality, traditional social norms and ultimately any concept of "God" at all. In an effort to reach lost people in this world system some have sacrificed not only the rule list, but the Biblical principles and sometimes even the Biblical truths that were the foundation of the list to begin with. Not only in many cases is the list gone, but also discarded with it is any standard of holiness that makes the Christian lifestyle distinctive. If that is not enough to concern you, consider that many of those "biblical non debatables" have now been debated and often done away with altogether. Few are left, most considered irrelevant or unenlightened; many dismissed entirely.

As the progression continues, I see the pendulum continuing it's swing.

I see something else though. Once again in my head I can hear Shaunda shouting, "All of life is not a song". Oh well, to me I think it might be! As I write this I also hear in my head the words to the beginning of the narration portion of Bill Gaither's "The Church Triumphant".

"God has always had a people..."

What is it that builds relationships among believers? What is it that makes musicians and athletes relationally close? Why can a gamer and a hunter sit beside each other in a room and find that common sense of purpose as they join in worship?

I am reminded of a sermon that my Pastor brought one Sunday morning years ago. It was incredibly simple and yet overtly profound at the same time. The entirety of the lesson for that day was summed up in one line. Borrowing that line from a movie current at the time, he proclaimed, "Keep the main thing, the main thing".

The unifying factor is being one in purpose. Another profound lesson for me from TEARS IN A BOTTLE comes rushing back: "It's not about me, it's all about God". He is the "main thing".

Regardless of our occupation, social standing, upbringing, race, gender, hobbies, political persuasion or any other defining factor, we all meet on common ground at the foot of the cross. But that is more than it appears on the outside, because it assuredly is an "inside thing". Although having Christ in your heart is the only requisite for Salvation, having Christ in *possession* of your heart is the prerequisite for personal relationship among Christ followers. Although we will never be perfect, this assures that Christ will be preeminent in our thoughts, actions and attitudes.

When Christ is in His rightful place in our heart, the place he literally died to purchase, He becomes the singular driving force in all of our life. So much of Him is at the very center of so much of us, that all other life factors are relatively inconsequential with regard to relationship. In other words, the hunting, fishing, policing, doctoring, biking, climbing, singing parts of us, though they may be a large part of what we do, are not supposed to be who we are.

You may ride a motorcycle, but if you are living from a personal center of pleasing Christ, you are really a Christ follower with a bike. If the motorcycle lifestyle determines your thoughts, actions and attitudes, we could probably not ever be close relationally. If Christ determines the position of our hearts, we likely could, provided you could ever get past the fact that I once owned a scooter.

The same is true in every situation. And for Shaunda and me, even at the beginnings of this Journey, we have found people all over this nation who share that singular passion for Christ. They are young and in big cities. They are old and in small rural areas. And these dynamics are interchangeable. Some still use a hymnal and sing the doxology. Others have media support and lighting that would rival a major concert production. Some wear shorts and t-shirts while others don coats and ties. Some meet in buildings constructed over a hundred years earlier while others don't meet in a building at all. Some carry their "physical church" with them in the back of pickups packaged in road cases.

But don't miss this: there are "churches" of every description that are most assuredly in the game. Yet there are "churches" of every description that have missed it all together. Too often holiness has been dumbed down in the name of relevancy to the point that a church ceases to be a church. This has nothing to do with size or any of the other current yardsticks some use to determine success. It has everything to do with an atmosphere of worship and life change that result in a personal holiness through trials that screams hope to a hurting world.

Some still hold to the rulebook in an effort to define Christianity by legalism. Others are still lost in a 70's rebellion (or 80's or 90's) against "anyone telling them what to do", even God. They are attempting to define Christianity by freedom. Unfortunately, their freedom looks a lot more like license. The legalist Christian demands assimilation while ignoring grace. The freedom Christian proclaims grace while denying holiness. Neither provide genuine hope.

Yet it may be this hope that is the foremost drawing force in Christianity. It signals to hurting people the message that there is something more, something deeper to hang on to and to identify with. And just look around. All people are hurting people.

We all need hope. Hope that our kids may someday get off drugs, that our husband will stop cheating, that the bank won't take the family home. We need hope to assure us that we can discover a purpose in life deeper than merely collecting toys and paying bills. A hope that tomorrow may indeed be better. We need to know that there is hope for something beyond this life, even when our child is dying of cancer before our very eyes; and we are powerless to enact change.

And for those who do not know Christ, there is no hope for their hopelessness. They may not even have discovered their hopelessness yet. They may be assuaging their pain with jet skis, softball leagues or a closet full of shoes. They may be masking it with alcohol or narcotics, legal or illegal. But don't be deceived. Hopelessness is always there, a constant companion every day.

Yet so is the hope. It is right there, every day with nail pierced hands outstretched proclaiming that we don't have to hide from our past or attempt to explain away our weakness. All we have to do is yield our heart to His presence. If that is you, reach out to someone who has that hope inside of him or her. They will share with you where that hope comes from. And I truly believe you can tell who they are.

On this Journey we have already seen many who define Christianity by exactly what it is, relationship. Relationship that is first with Christ, and then with each other. I believe that our country is full of people who are getting it right. I have met many who share my passion, who share my drive and who share a belief that this message of hope in Christ is that only real answer for a soul destined for a hopeless eternity.

These are fellow Journeyers who have no need for any list to tell them how to live in the name of legalism, nor do they need to make an apology for lifestyle choices made in the name of freedom. They are people with whom we can genuinely pray, and who take their role in life as a purveyor of hope seriously. Their pendulum doesn't move. It is attached squarely to the completed work of Christ and the infallible word of God.

I am especially grateful today to have just such a person right by my side.

Wow, maybe Shaunda is right. I do talk too much. At least writing this today might give her a pleasant ride tomorrow when she is once more "stuck in the truck". I just hope she doesn't wear that silly t-shirt... again.

THE GREATER JOURNEY...

When you get right down to it, we can live without a lot of things. We can live without possessions. We can live without a fancy car. We can live without the acclaim of others. There is however, something we just can't live without... hope.

> Pr 13:12
> Hope deferred makes the heart sick, but a longing fulfilled is a tree of life.

Read...
and look for the word "hope". See what you can learn about hope from each of these verses.

> 1 Co 29:14, 15
> Job 8:13
> Job 13;15
> Ps 25:21
> Ps 31:24
> Ps 33:17-22

Now that you have the idea, keep going. Use a concordance or a Bible search engine. See what God says about hope. Oh yeah, grab a cup of coffee. This is going to take a while!

CHAPTER 17
A View From The Vista

Hard to believe, but half of our "North of the Red River" tour is now behind us and we are beginning a new and different phase of the journey. The first half of this tour (as with the entirety of "Chasing Spring") has held unexpected but hoped for and welcome blessings. Every Church we have shared Matt's story with (except one) has invited us to come back on YEAR 2 of our Journey. The singular exception held some extenuating circumstances, but we had an amazing service. I'm betting we could go back there as well.

This wonderful blessing has created a situation that calls for a little "detour of focus". This "detour" to me, is really something God may have planned all along. For some reason there were a few dates in the middle of this tour for which we did not have places to tell Matt's story, and these Sundays are all back-to-back. As the return opportunities started coming in, it became obvious that I would need a different story to tell when we return next year. I considered these two facts simultaneously and suddenly realized that this "break in the action" was not to be simply a time to sit and relax.

Preparing for a worship service like "The Greater Journey Live Worship Event" and the new one (whatever it ends up being called) is a time and creative intensive process to say the least. First of all, a theme has to be determined. It then requires the establishment of a service flow and the creation of all the audio and video media to support it. The final assembly and quality control calls for yet another few days. Our initial planning had already led us to Colorado. What better place than the mountains of Colorado to seek God and perhaps provide some creative inspiration as well?

At the same time I am planning to make every effort to complete book #2. As many of you may recall, I told you that the "On the Virge, The Journey Of A Lifetime" blog may be book #3 (if it ever becomes a book that is). The second effort bears the working title "Stories From The Road, Lessons From Life and Death". Soon my "On The Virge" blog will likely include excerpts from this work as well as I turn my attention in that direction. So it is in this phase of the Journey that I find myself this morning, at the beginning of a slower pace, at least as far as mileage is concerned.

A "byway" is defined as a small side road not regularly used by people or traffic. A byway often parallels the interstate, yet offers more opportunity for enjoying a few vistas. It is often the "old highway" and provides a glimpse of yesterday, when life's pace was much slower and much simpler. This is where I sit today while I gaze on the surrounding mountains and enjoy the mid 70's temperature even though it is late July. While travelling on some of this nation's byways over the past months, we have learned to watch for scenic pullouts. They usually afford gorgeous views of mountains, valleys or plains. These are vistas that you would never have the opportunity to appreciate if you keep your eyes fixed on the road and your foot planted on the gas.

Sorry to argue with pre-conceived opinions held by most of us non-Kansans, but Kansas is not flat and ugly; well, at least not Central and Eastern Kansas. As a matter of fact, we took a drive down a designated scenic highway between two north central Kansas towns that was designated the "Western Vistas Historic Byway". While these views may not rival the breathtaking overlooks of the Smoky Mountains, the Skyline Drive or the Blue Ridge Parkway, they were nonetheless surprisingly beautiful. You could literally see for miles, horizon to horizon.

Here are a few other observations from the Journey that were a bit surprising to us, and perhaps will be to you as well. There are mountains in Texas. Real mountains, rugged mountains, beautiful mountains. Colorado has deserts. Real deserts, rugged deserts, ugly deserts! Here's some more: Kansas is not entirely flat. Indiana has "hills" that to me looked just as steep as the "mountains" in some other states. They all have some interesting bridges to navigate, ask Shaunda. Please ask Shaunda! To me, the unique fascination has been how different our nation can look through the same windshield. And how different it actually is from our preconceived notions.

Looking back from today's vista, I realize that each telling of our story was likewise different. In complete disclosure, there are several versions of the story although 90% of the content of the service remains the same.   One telling of the story concludes with an introspective tone.   I have an alternate ending that brings the experience full circle with the addition of some up-tempo worship tunes. I speak at two different times in the presentation, which offers some latitude as well.

I try to employ what seems to be the best approach for each group of people; the best way to tailor our message of hope. Why, I've even taken this to the extreme of purchasing a suit and tie, and I've worn it on two occasions so far.   I simply don't want the message of the story to be mitigated by musical style or even how the storyteller is dressed.

Even with these factors considered, each telling of the story is mostly different because each group of worshippers is different. We have experienced worship services where the response could be easily measured in thunderous applause and shouts of praise.   Others have held response better measured by gasps, flowing tears and warm embraces.   Still others have met with a sort of stunned silence and an overwhelming movement of product from the table.

All, yes every one so far, has met with what has been for me an unusual presence of the Spirit of God. Spending nearly a lifetime in the ministry I have learned that this is the necessary commodity for genuine lifechange. Neither the style of music presented nor the style of the messenger's wardrobe is of true importance.   These minute details pale in comparison to the necessity of the presence of God. I am not a good enough musician and certainly not a good enough orator to change anyone's life.   Then again, no one is. Any good that is found coming from this messenger can be traced directly back to goodness of God.

Our last stop before the halfway point in this part of the Journey was a small church in north central Kansas. This presentation, as with all the others, promised to be mostly the same, yet entirely different. This small fellowship of believers included a family who had lost a child seven months earlier. They had also experienced two funerals in the past week. As you might imagine, this created a unique environment for a much needed message of hope.

Between opportunities to tell the story, I have kept busy with other aspects of our new ministry. I've been privileged to remotely produce a weekly Texas radio show as well as produce media and consult on another radio show. I have been able to produce media for another Church and even edit and brand Spanish worship videos for another, at least I think that is what I did. This last church however, presented me with an opportunity to consult in media as well as work with their musicians in some basic theory and worship planning. These opportunities produced both intended and unintended consequences.

I was able to assist in establishing at least a plan of how they might improve their projection system to better utilize media and lyric projection. I was able to help them understand how to improve their audio assets. I was also able to provide input in service planning including layering, hard stops, soft stops and the elimination of dead air. All of these were intended consequences.

I did not however, realize how getting to know these people before the Sunday telling of the story would affect how I approached it. Of those I worked with, there was the one young man whose very demeanor shouted stability. There was another whose energy was contagious to all around. There was yet another who was reserved, yet his hidden value to a music ministry soon became apparent. Then there was the pianist. She was talented, committed and willing to learn. Shaunda also got to spend some time with her as well as they shared a common experience. Shaunda gave her a book.

That Sunday morning found me even more desirous than usual for an outpouring of God's grace on these people. I guess I was more aware of the place of great need in which I found myself. Getting to know more about the people to whom I would minister, and then to share with them as they expressed a desire to make their Church great and support their Pastor only seemed to deepen my desire to minister. I left with a strange, deep desire to see that body of believers flourish.

That morning also reminded me of the futility of trying to accomplish the work of God in my own power. This service, like the view out the windshield, was different than all the others. Yet, like the others, was equally blessed with the presence of God. Good thing. That lets me off the hook. I did those things I could do. God did all those things I could not. The latter are the truly important ones.

So here I sit, looking out the rear window of the truck for a moment, grateful for all the miles and all the blessings and experiences. Looking back to the windshield I see a few days physically jammed in an overcrowded RV park in Colorado. And for that I am truly grateful. Interesting how beautiful the scenery is, and even much more so when shared with friends. The first week of this byway you see, is shared with friends, and even a musketeer.

What a joy to take the byway, to slow down and savor the Journey; to enjoy the *view from the vista.*

THE GREATER JOURNEY...

So what's your rush? Let's try an experiment. Ready? Here we go.

Don't read ahead; don't turn the page, just count to 250. Go ahead.

How long did that take? It depends on how fast you spoke the numbers, but this could likely be measured in a single digit number of minutes.

Now answer this question...
> *At any time this week did you devote at least that much time in deliberate, uninterrupted focused communication with God?*

In times past the average attention span was measured in hours. And then came television. With its influence we began to think of life in terms of hours, and soon in half hours.

Enter into the equation what we call social media. Today you have just about 5 seconds to get your message heard. After that people are on to the next post or tweet. Who knows what the future holds? Someday a person may read these words and realize that yet another outside force has altered our thought process once again.

What urgent things can you remove from your schedule so you will make time for what is truly important; a genuine walk with God.

What else is so important? Take a moment. Enjoy the view. You may be amazed at what you discover.

Like I said: What's your rush?

CHAPTER 18
The Summit

Today I finished a mountaintop climb that began more than 20 years ago.

Seriously. I made it to the very top; the Summit. This was not the highest mountain in the world, or even the highest in the County I am in for that matter. Yet at more than 12,000 feet it's the highest mountain I have ever climbed. To say the least, it was breathtaking in every imaginable way.

I remember the morning that this climb first began. It was at a small motel with an adjoining restaurant somewhere in the Northeast. It was during a family vacation when Joe Jr's age could likely have been counted on the fingers of one of my hands. Hard to believe that in three days from today, Lord willing, I will have the privilege of joining him and his sweet wife for his thirty-second birthday.

On that morning so many years ago we had just walked the few steps from our hotel room to eat breakfast at the tiny restaurant attached to the motel. We were seated next to a window. As we were waiting to order, I remember looking out that window and noticing a small hill on some adjacent vacant land. It was not an impressive hill by anyone's standard and in no way to be confused with a real mountain. It was high enough however, to warrant a quick challenge from Dad:

"Hey kids, after we order, do you want to climb a mountain?"

Tiny eyes began dancing and impatient fidgeting and smiles of anticipation now replaced the morning's whines and pleas of "don't make me get up yet". Amazing how the challenge of a mountaintop experience (even if in reality it is only a small hill) can quickly exhaust a child's limited supply of patience. If that seems like an unreasonable premise to you, just imagine how overwhelming a small hill can appear when you are very small yourself.

Today's climb however, was the real thing. The hill was indeed a mountain, the small boy now a full-grown man. The Dad? He was easily recognized as the older guy fighting for every breath, compliments of the thin mountain air and a few too many pounds. Scampering the last 20 feet or so to the rocky point with an ease that made the Dad a bit jealous, the son summited. He then turned and stood ready to create a video record of Dad's first summit experience.

 After a few minutes of reveling and enjoying life at the top of the world (at least for me), and after the event was crowned with photos, videos, high fives and the obligatory signing of the log, we began the unforgiving trek down. I'll admit that I was looking for every excuse to pause and catch my breath by making conversation; when I could actually speak out loud that is. A few hundred feet into the descent when the terrain leveled a bit, the topic turned to kids, memories and yes, even that "mountaintop experience" from all those years ago.

Funny how time turns the tables on us. I was no longer in the lead, holding out the aura of a junior summit experience while actually only climbing a hill. This time I found myself (more times than I'd like to admit) the distant straggler. Years ago my heart filled with joy as I trekked to the top of the hill with that small hand in mine conquering the "mountain" of that day. How blessed I feel today to have been given the privilege to once again relive those moments.

There is one more piece of today's puzzle that made this triumph even more special. Joe Jr. and his lovely wife Tacha are expecting their first child. Another generation, another moment in time, perhaps even another mountain, or at least a hill, to summit.

Funny as well, how sometimes the events of years past seem to have taken place so long ago. Often they seem like they took place in a different lifetime. Others are nearly or completely forgotten altogether. Then there are yet other times that it almost seems as if time is merely a fabric that can easily be folded end to end and then connected by a single thread.

At every step (and every slide) down the mountain it seemed that scenes from different decades readily interposed themselves in my mind. For a few moments it was today with the Colorado sun blazing on the back of my neck. Then in the fraction of a second it was yesterday, and in my mind that small boy's hand was once again clasped tightly in mine.

Can you sense why this is truly the "Journey of a Lifetime" for me?

Thank you Lord.

THE GREATER JOURNEY...

What have been the "summit" experiences of your life?

What if today when your phone rings, it is the doctor's office? There is bad news. Your life that you thought somehow would go on forever now has a time period attached to it. Three months or three years. Perhaps it is not your life in the balance, but the life of someone you love more than your own life.

What would you do differently? What choices would you make with the next few moments? What unsaid things would you say? What undone things would you do? What sin that you hold on to so tightly would you rush to repent of?

Read James 4:13, 14

Why do we treat the gift of time so callously when we have no promise of tomorrow? Of even the next breath...

Would you rethink the definition of those "summits"? The description of what is truly important?

CHAPTER 19
Tourist Trap

We all know what a tourist trap is. We've learned that lesson. Some of us have learned it more than once.

I mentioned "snake farms" and such in the TEARS IN A BOTTLE Study Guide as well as in STORIES FROM THE ROAD. These types of "businesses" including giant "jackelopes" and gift shops of every description were the staples of Historic Route 66 as well as other highways that crisscrossed the United States. As children, they were so much a part of the summer vacation experience that they somehow weaved their way into required stops for today's modern road trip. While you may still occasionally find a working snake farm, most have faded into history along with the paint on the few remaining structures that once housed these and other overtly American "treasures". What are these "treasures"? We called them tourist traps.

There were at least three things these roadside attractions had in common. First, they had a similar "carnival" sort of appeal. Cheesy roadside attractions often included offerings that ran the gambit from mere oddity to borderline macabre. After all, must we really pay a financial premium to gaze on a buffalo with more than the prescribed number of heads?

Speaking of "paying a premium", that was the second thing they also seemed to have in common. They were priced so high that parting with the cash often brought about a less than civil outburst from my Father. In spite of the exorbitant fee for admission, the yearly family road trip seemed always to include more than one of these adventures. This was likely because of the third thing they shared in common. They were marketed at young children in such a manner that guaranteed an outcry within the small confines of the family car. Outcries similar to "Please, Dad, please! I've never ridden a jackelope before!"

Tourist trap. You know what I mean. Ever paid $8 for a breakfast of reconstituted eggs and toast? How about $20 for a $5 t-shirt? Got a collection of saltshakers, shot glasses or toothpick holders stuffed in a box somewhere? Own a chunk of petrified wood or a piece of an actual meteor? How about a seashell or living seahorse? Tourist trap.

Now don't be misled. Although the paint is peeling from the many of the stucco buildings on abandoned stretches of our highways, the art of "fishing for children" is alive and well. On our recent trip to Branson Missouri, I experienced it first hand when our Granddaughter came across a slick advertising brochure offering promises of incredible animal acts. I dropped Grandma off at the theater, wide-eyed granddaughter in tow, while I headed for an entertainment mecca more of my own liking: a car wash.

After two hours of washing, waxing and polishing bliss I returned to the theatre to retrieve my passengers.

Granddaughter was aglow with stories of incredible feats performed by a diverse cast of animals. Grandma, on the other hand, returned with rolling eyes explaining that most of the performing animals depicted on that advertising slick were replaced by common housecats.

Me? I found myself missing enough cash to have covered a dinner for two at a steakhouse, not even taking into consideration the sixteen quarters I fed the coin machine at the car wash. Oh well, the smile on the tired little girl's face that night made it seem worth it. Still I said to myself: "Tourist Trap", just as sure as if I had just spent two hours at a snake farm.

Over the past few weeks we have been holed up in central Colorado. I have taken advantage of a lull in the opportunity to present Matt's story by recording, writing, arranging and producing video for year two's opportunities. I might add that I have actually worked very hard. And in the spirit of full disclosure, I have played very hard as well. If you're not sure what I mean by that, please re-read "The Summit".

Truth is, we have spent the last two weeks at a beautiful National Recreation Area surrounded by mountains, mesas and Caribbean blue colored waters. We are in close proximity to Joe Jr. and his wife Tacha.

This has afforded some amazing opportunities. To be quite honest, I'm not sure when I have laughed as much as I have in the past few days. It almost seems that the laughter is as good as medicine. Hmm… seems like I've heard that somewhere before.

I have watched Joe(y) play shortstop for his softball team (talk about bringing back memories) and we have celebrated our birthdays. For my birthday, we spent an entire day on an alpine lake searching for trout. I did the searching, Shaunda did the driving and Joe and Tacha did the finding.

We all went home that night and Joe Jr. did the cleaning. Joe Jr. and Tacha did the cooking and then we all did the eating. Talk about fresh fish!

In planning ahead, Joe and Tacha took a couple days off work and we all enjoyed a mini vacation. It started with a 2-mile hike followed by a National Park Service boat tour into the Black Canyon of the Gunnison with 2000-foot tall cliffs towering on either side. That was followed by a picnic lunch overlooking a roaring Colorado River. Then it was on to see the Black Canyon of the Gunnison National Park from the topside and then to Montrose and an evening at a drive-in movie. Yes, a drive in theatre still exists in Montrose Colorado. And yes they were playing an animated feature that night, and no, it didn't really matter. It was a genuine blast from the past.

Following a scrumptious (?) hotel breakfast of pancakes prepared entirely by a machine, we headed for a breathtaking mountain drive to Ouray Colorado and beyond through Colorado mining country. There were "waterfall viewing" stops for Shaunda and "old abandoned mining operation" stops for me, all courtesy of our well-prepared tour guides. The crowning jewel of the day was to be our final stop in Ridgeway, Colorado. Why was this an important stop for me? Glad you asked!

I am a man of true grit.

Well, at least a man who loves the movie, the original that is; the 1969 version. The book from which the movie was made was set in the Winding Stair Mountains of Arkansas. The main town in the book was Fort Smith Arkansas. Enter into this equation the "reality" of Hollywood. This John Wayne classic would be shot in the San Juan Mountains of Colorado. The town that would stand in for Fort Smith? You guessed it. Ridgeway.

And what a stop it was. Chen Lee's house was still there as was the mortuary where little Mattie saw her father laid out. The "Fort Smith" saloon remains although it actually sells only clothes and notions. Down the sidewalk was the building that stood in for "Hanging Judge Parker's" courtroom. The town park that once held the gallows is intact complete with easily recognizable trees and rocks. The train depot is there (except that it really always was a house). On the horizon, chimney rock (prominent in several scenes including the final shootout) is readily recognizable. Even the actual prison wagon that Sheriff Rooster Cogburn makes his first appearance with is readily available for inspection. Although it sits empty in its final resting place of honor, I could still hear the rattling of the prisoner's chains. And if you somehow don't really understand any of that, I am truly sorry! You have missed a huge piece of genuine Americana.

And lunch... did I mention lunch? Why the "True Grit Café" of course. Honestly, just the name was enough for me. The fact that in Colorado you could order sweet tea and chicken fried anything was nearly enough to make me shout "hooray for Texas".

I had done my homework too. I knew all of this glory awaited me at the end of the mountain drive, and so I waited patiently. Patiently, that is until midway through the drive when the sign for Box Canyon Falls appeared on the right. Did I say run down, faded sign? I knew right away what this was.

"Never been there," Joe Jr. said. "Wanna go?"

Before I could say "John Wayne still lives in my heart" Shaunda had blurted out an emphatic "yes".

We turned down the dirt road (path might be a better descriptive word) and almost immediately saw another sign: "Admission $4".   My dear departed Dad was screaming in my left ear. In my right ear I heard the snickering of the Branson housecats that had recently stolen my night out at the steakhouse.   It was then I could contain myself no longer.   With nearly the passion I have experienced only during some recent sermon I screamed "TOURIST TRAP"!

I thought surely that my astute observation (that the others had obviously missed) would produce the desired response. "You are so right" they would say. "How could we have missed it? Let's leave here right now and head for John Wayne/True Grit heaven."
Instead, they ignored me, chuckled amongst themselves and headed directly towards the man who would soon be "stealing" more of my cash. Now $16 poorer, I followed last in line. $16 is not a large amount of cash for sure, but it would have bought both

Shaunda and me our own orders of those reconstituted eggs and toast.

Then almost instantly feeling a bit childish, I conjured up my best smile and joined in for the short 500-foot walk. The landscape at the beginning did absolutely nothing to prepare me for what was to come. This was a short walk into an amazingly beautiful canyon. Ducking quite low to avoid the sharp rocks protruding from the top precariously close to my head we all heard the unmistakable roar of a powerful waterfall that was suddenly near.

I won't describe the location further; the photographs will cover that nicely. I will say that during the next few moments God used this simple experience to reinforce a powerful lesson.

Life, even when lived to the best of our ability to honor Christ, still holds difficulties and distressing experiences. Sometimes as we live through these, we might bristle a bit. Other times we cover up; even build walls. We might place ourselves in an emotional state where we create a fortress, completely surrounding us, determining to never allow ourselves to be hurt again.

We might even lock ourselves up emotionally so tightly that when we are presented by opportunities that would bring joy, we instead read the signs and determine it to be just another trap. We decide not to even take the risk, deciding in advance that the cost will be too great. And we head on down the road, sadly never realizing what we have just missed.

And so to life we scream... "It's a trap". Run. Don't take the risk. Cover up. Life will never be any better. I'll never make it. I'll just be hurt again. Get back in the car and drive away.

And then I realized... what if I had not taken *this* small risk, opened my wallet and handed over that insignificant amount of cash. I would have missed one of the most beautiful natural wonders I have ever seen. Worse yet I would likely have traded these precious moments with my family for a couple of plates of reconstituted eggs.

We stayed quite a long time at the canyon today, and I was glad to do it. When it was finally time to move on, I was no longer in a hurry. My time in Ridgeway could wait.

Leaving the canyon, my son took this photo. I've entitled it "The Four of Us". Come on Joe, there are only three in the picture " you say? Well look again. There's Shaunda, our daughter-in-law Tacha, and me... and our next Grandchild on the way.

Dear God, it is at times like these that there are once again just not enough words in our language to say thank You. Thank You for the John Wayne days. Thank You as well for the tourist traps. Thank You that when so many times I wanted to just run away, often because of my own failures, that I instead found my "true grit" in you. Thank You most of all that while I sit here tonight in the darkness with a couple of leaky eyes, I can rejoice in the simple things.

Simple things like the fact that I literally walked miles over the last four days beside that little guy who used to wear the big bird clothes (got to listen to vintage Joe Knight tunes to get that one). And that tonight I have the love of my life at arms length, and I can hear her breathe. And the reality that I spent irreplaceable, once in a lifetime moments today with my daughter-in-law who bears in her body a new life. A life that God willing, will one day speak the word "Poppi".

You see, earlier today when we all held hands over a chicken fried steak overlooking John Wayne heaven, asking God's blessings on our food and pledging to never again take one moment of life for granted, the lesson became clear. May we always realize that the simple things in life are most often the very best things. We are just pilgrims on this Journey, tourists if you will. Please help me avoid one of the worst tourist traps of all; missing the joy for fear of taking the risk.

Thank you Lord that today I didn't miss the canyon.

THE GREATER JOURNEY...

Sometimes we say we want to "please God"; but do we really?

Read Hebrews 11:1-6

I fear that one of the biggest mistakes of this life is when we begin to believe that we have God all figured out. Many fellow Journeyers have become discouraged when they equate the unexplainable nature of an Almighty God with the unforgivable actions of one of His human servants.

The danger here is found in putting God "in a box". When tragedy comes and our world closes in on us, our "God" is just not big enough to lead through the wilderness.

Please don't be offended by any shock value in the next statement. This is something I was told once when I asked a friend to help me understand what God was doing in my life. He responded:

"I wouldn't give you two cents for a god that could be explained all the time."

Give it some thought and see what you think. If God were so easily comprehended, would we ever need faith? If we never had faith could we ever fully please Him?

K S

CHAPTER 20
Intentional Darkness

When you truly share a relationship with someone, you want them to be proud of you. I yearn for Shaunda's admiration. I want my children to be proud of me, my friends to respect me. Simply stated, I want all of these people to be pleased with me.

I have these friends you see. One of which you've heard about if you've read TEARS IN A BOTTLE (He might be a "Musketeer"), the other a retired businessman, and still others who are a part of the "Men of Monday Morning". You'll hear more from them soon.

While having varied backgrounds, we do share some things in common. We all went to church together, they have all played vital roles in this "Journey of a Lifetime", and at one time or another they have all laughed at me. Not the "making fun of me" kind of laugh. It was more of the "I've got a little different view of what's going on here than you do" kind of chuckle.

All of these men were my confidants during the formative stages of this Journey, and at one time or another I gleaned valuable wisdom and insight from each of them.

If you recall, for me this Journey started several years before "YEAR 1". It first began in my heart; in that place where only you and God can see. Soon I shared the vision with Shaunda, and then it came time to bring close friends into the discussion; enter the Musketeer and the Businessman. Very soon thereafter the Men of Monday Morning came alongside as well. Sprinkled amongst their encouragement, listening skills and invaluable advice over the next months there seemed always to be a chuckle now and then.

Their smiles typically appeared when I discussed the future of this endeavor. For whatever reason, from inception (and continuing to the present) I have stated I have only been given vision for two years. I had no idea what might come beyond that. Sitting here today towards the end of YEAR 1, I can say that I still have no idea. I also had no idea of what to expect when we first started the truck, hooked up The Virge and headed down the highway. When I discussed this in advance with my friends, it seemed they always had a word of encouragement... and that recurring smile.

Early on in my ministry I heard a Pastor make a statement that so impacted me that I still remember it today. He challenged us to "never use the word sacrifice when we give up anything for Him who gave up everything". So please know I don't consider the following a tremendous sacrifice in any way.

Perspective is one of those keys to successful living. From a certain perspective we gave up many things to start down this path. As I often say at the beginning of the LIVE WORSHIP EVENT, "please pray for my wife. Women are funny. When you quit your job, sell their house and all their "stuff" and move into a fifth wheel they tend to get a little nervous". That line usually gets a laugh or two (as intended), yet it also shines a little light into the beginnings of our Journey.

It is true that at a certain level (the emotional level, that is) doing whatever this is that we're doing takes a measure of faith. It is likewise true that on a different level (the spiritual level) it is not really that big of a deal since it calls for relatively little faith. It all comes down to perspective. If my perspective is on worldly things, I must exercise a fair amount of faith. If my perspective is on better things, it matters only where I place my faith; or better said; in Whom I place my faith.

God, you see, has been faithful to me all of my life, even in the darkness when I (like David) could not even see the path that lay one step ahead. At times, God is like a kind of "spiritual altimeter" if you will. My IFR pilot friends will maneuver their plane to an effortless landing (effortless from a novice's point of view that is) even if the runway is not visible until just before tires touch concrete; if even then. They have learned, and model for that matter, some valuable Christian life lessons. When flying in conditions that prohibit the use of your vision, trust your instruments. Don't circle until you run out of fuel waiting for the fog to clear. Watch those gauges, communicate with the tower and then just land the plane.

Now may I be real honest here? Leaving my last church ministry after 21 years was not an easy decision. Since Shaunda and I have East Texas as our home base, we still see many of these great people we served with when we are there. But that's just not the same as being together every week and sharing life's Journey. I have even longed for our little home in Greenville while the winds of a Kansas thunderstorm violently rocked The Virge on a Church parking lot.

I can tell you though, that this Journey has been a joy well beyond anything I could have ever dreamed, and in every imaginable way. The beautiful country we have experienced; the amazing power of God we have witnessed; and the ability to place my head on my pillow at night (or on the headrest in the truck) and sense that Shaunda and I are never really alone.

Yesterday I was heading to an early morning breakfast with one of those folks I mentioned earlier. While driving to my favorite breakfast spot a strange thought process enveloped me. I remembered a very significant moment in this Journey two weeks earlier while heading back to the Virge. We had just experienced a string of some of the greatest services yet, and also in every imaginable way. In a few moments of relative quiet, without warning Shaunda uncharacteristically went very deep.

"You know Joe", she began, "If we never travel another mile or sing in one more church, this has been worth it."

I shared this story at breakfast that morning, and guess what? I got that chuckle and a smile. It seems that God's incredible blessings are no surprise to those who have partnered with us on this Journey, yet to Shaunda and me they appear unannounced and often quite unexpected. Sometimes it is like having Christmas morning over and over, and not being sure if this will be the day it comes around once again. I understand the chuckles and smiles now. They are saying that they are not surprised. To some degree, they saw this coming when I did not.

I started this chapter by pointing out that when we truly share a relationship with someone, we want them to be proud of us. We yearn for admiration. We want our children to be proud of us, our friends to respect us. I likewise want all of these people to be pleased with me, but most of all, I want God to be pleased with me.

I agree with Shaunda. This crazy Journey has all been worth it already. As a matter of fact, had I known that the payoff would be many times the price of admission; this Journey would have required little or no faith at all.

But then again, without faith, God would not have been pleased with me. You see, without faith it is impossible to please Him. Covering the few miles to the local breakfast spot this morning waiting for the sun to rise I couldn't help but wonder: Does God ever provide for us an intentional darkness? An intentional darkness that requires faith on our part. The faith we can exercise just so He may be pleased with us?

Here's a thought. Embrace the darkness on your Journey. Trust your spiritual altimeter. Don't simply circle aimlessly in bitterness until you run out of fuel. Watch those gauges. Communicate with the Father and land the plane.

And remember, the darkness does not last forever. The sun will rise again. If not in this world, then assuredly in the next. There is a place with no more sorrow, no more pain, no more hurt, no more tears…

…and no more death.

THE GREATER JOURNEY…

In a moment of crisis or trial, no one truly likes to be completely alone. Here's something I love to do when looking at scripture. Take each word of the following familiar verse, and focus on them one at a time. Consider each word individually, analyze each meaning and apply it personally to you.

See if perhaps today the last half of this verse (or another approached similarly) might speak to you in a unique way.

Hebrews 13:5b
    …Never will I leave you;
            never will I forsake you.

CHAPTER 21
We May Never Pass This Way Again

YEAR 1 on this "Journey of a Lifetime" is about to take its final turn. (By the way, you can relax. I think I may nearly be out of these cheesy "life is a highway" metaphors.) Today we finished our last out of state presentation of Matt's story for this year. In a few hours we will once again point the Virge south towards our home state of Texas. The next four weekend's events are all within driving distance of our home base. Add to that a singular Christmas concert in December and YEAR 1 will be in the books.

Once again, today's telling of the story was nearly exactly the same, and yet entirely different. A venue with an excellent sound system, a fine grand piano and good acoustical properties added a special touch of enjoyment to the presenter. The supernatural moving of God however, assured that the impact would be deeply felt and long lasting.

What has become a "typical event day" repeated itself. Today's service time was lengthened by a service element specific to this particular Church family as well as by a longer than normal response time. All these elements combined brought the entire time from downbeat to dismissal to nearly ninety minutes. The next ninety minutes were filled with talking to people, sharing encouragement and hearing their stories. It seems that we have spent as much (or more) time talking with people than we do telling the story. And believe me, we are good with that.

Once again we heard stories of people's heartache and struggles that were almost mind-boggling. I am very aware of the fact that the emotional pain of one person's Journey cannot be honestly compared with that of another's. Yet on this day, Shaunda and I would hear from no less than three families with whom I would not wish to change places. I would not dare tell even one detail of the things told to me, but I assure you these families are worthy of your prayers.

There was yet another story I heard today however, that I gained permission from the family to share. You may recall that I wrote earlier of the three basic themes of the Live Worship Event. First, this is a story of hope. Second, it answers the question "Can God be Trusted? Finally it concludes with a challenge to "Never take one moment of life for granted". I think that this family's story beautifully illustrates all three.

The Worship Pastor of this Church is a good deal younger than me. He was a most gracious host and a highly skilled partner in the technical aspects required for the presentation. In preparing for this day's event, we had shared several preparatory conversations via text message and telephone. Interspersed in these contacts was the opportunity for me to discover that he had experienced a life Journey quite similar to mine.

We both had chosen the path of vocational ministry. We both are musicians and have served as Worship Pastors. This young man had been married to a woman who was diagnosed with cancer in the very same month and year that Matt was. His marriage was destined for an unfortunate and untimely end with her death, just a few months after Matt's. We surely had experienced similar Journeys with similar heartache.

Yet we also have enjoyed the indescribable healing hand of God in our lives. My new friend has likewise discovered that in spite of the pain, God can surely be trusted in life's darkest hours. He has experienced the hope that is found by embracing a life of brokenness and watch it mended by the Giver of Life. You see today I also go to meet the wonderful woman to whom he is now married.

It would seem that this young lady has a story all her own to tell as well, although she can't quite remember all the beginnings of it. Her story played out when she was only three years old. It was then that she was diagnosed with Lymphoma…non-Hodgkin's Lymphoma that is…the very same type of cancer that afflicted Matt. This picture is of her and Shaunda.

Now I don't want to sugar coat this at all, this couple's lives are full of continued physical struggles. They have learned another harsh lesson about cancer. The truth is that in many cases cancer can truly be cured…if the cure itself doesn't kill you. Although there are lingering physical problems for her, she has indeed been one of the fortunate ones to be declared cured. As a matter of fact, her doctors have told her that they genuinely believe she may be the first...the *very* first...to ever be cured of this particular type of cancer.

And that leads us to the third point... I guess both of us worship guys shared a few moments together today "not taking one moment of life for granted". I told my readers in TEARS IN A BOTTLE, that I wrote not so I could forget, but rather so I could remember. I want to always remember the precious gift that I have been given with the dawn of each new day.

I was blessed with wonderful parents; parents who took me to church and taught me that a relationship with Christ was the singular most important thing in my life. More important than friends, more important than money, more important than earthly success. I would love to pick up the phone and give them a quick call to tell them one more time how grateful I am. These days I have finally realized exactly how great of a gift I was given. It's just that I can't call them ever again. There are no phone lines in heaven.

Only two weeks ago on the way to Missouri (where we are today), Shaunda and I spent a few days in Oklahoma. A few days at the same state park where I wrote a portion of TEARS IN A BOTTLE, and the same state park where we often took the kids for a quick getaway because of its close proximity to the Dallas/Forth Worth metroplex.

The first night we were there (now two weeks ago) Shaunda and I drove to one of our favorite spots. It overlooks a beautiful lake and earthen dam. As we sat in the fading twilight in near silence my mind drifted back to an earlier time. I looked down on the very spot where the boys took off their shoes and raced down the rocky hillside to jump into the water. It was then that the silence was assailed, as it seemed I could hear the laughter and the playful voices of three boys echoing off the distant shoreline as they splashed and played in the water on that hot summer's day. The voices of three boys: Joey, Brian... and Matt.

The brisk fall breeze summoned me back to reality almost against my will. I turned to Shaunda and said: "Do you remember..."

Before I could even finish the question she replied "yes".

The silence returned, this time accompanied by an occasional warm, salty drip on my cheek. I really wouldn't mind living at least a part of that summer day just once more, but I cannot. Time has moved steadily on, passing by unforgiving and relentless, just like the passing white lines painted on the interstate highway concrete. (Well how about that! I believe I did have at least one more "life is a highway" metaphor left!)

Do you find yourself trapped by the routines of daily living? Have you allowed life's circumstances to drain from you the ability simply to get up and get out? Does bitterness hold you at bay with its cold stare of death? Are you tormented by your failures or held in chains by your fears? Has the merciless onslaught of loneliness stripped you of your joy?

What a shame when we allow our joy to be stolen away while all the time somewhere in the distance we can hear the incessant ticking of a clock. A clock counting the seconds of our lives as they slip away. Some of you reading this need to take a moment and just step back.   Lay your burdens at the feet of Jesus for "He cares for you". Leave them there. Get up and go on, and don't look over your shoulder. Throw both of your hands in the air as an act of surrender…and of worship.

Make a phone call, send an email, drop an instant message. Drive across the city, the county, the state, the nation. Do whatever you must to make things right by those you have offended…and forgive those who have offended you. And don't get the two mixed up. Perhaps harder still, make certain your heart of repentance assures you that God has forgiven you and then make the most difficult of all the steps of forgiveness… forgive yourself.

It's time to renew your hope in the God who can be trusted. It's time to lean in, get up and engage life once again. It's time to realize that we must never take one moment of this life for granted. Realize that once a moment of time is spent, no change is ever given. Exercise the tremendous power that abides in your choice. We may never pass this way again.

To be honest, I have regretted many decisions and many actions in my life. But today I do not regret one moment I have spent in prayer or in worship. I don't regret one game of little league baseball or softball I have watched or coached. I don't regret one fishing trip, one vacation, one bike ride, one game of nerf basketball (while the snow could be seen against the bright driveway light out of Joey's bedroom window), one game night, one Max's movie theatre, one whiffle ball or tennis baseball game (we made that one up), one hike or one afternoon of defending the fort at the park while being "attacked" by small children with imaginary weapons.

And I don't regret one mile we have travelled, metaphorically and literally.

As I write this, the new day began a little more than two hours ago. Now that I have shared these words with you, perhaps my "mile a minute" brain will find some breathing room and I can convince it to close down for the night. Shaunda is asleep all the way on the other end of the house. OK... Shaunda is asleep a little less than thirty feet away on the other end of the fifth wheel. I hope I don't wake her when I slip quietly into bed; she tends to be a bit fussy when I do.

It's just that I have to tell her one more time how much I love her. I have to let her know how grateful I am for having just shared with her one of the greatest years of my life. Or I can wait and tell her tomorrow when I wake up... *but what if tomorrow never comes or I don't wake up?* Both are genuine possibilities.

Besides, she just has to know that I have not taken a single mile of this Journey of a Lifetime for granted.

Well how about that! I guess I had yet another one of those "life is a highway" metaphors way back in there somewhere. Wanna bet I find some more?

THE GREATER JOURNEY...

What if tonight was the very last night of your life?

CHAPTER 22
Foundation

When I travel I am a ridiculously meticulous planner. Mapping programs, travel guides, campground review websites and online reservations are my best friends. I have also learned however, that some of the greatest experiences we have enjoyed have been those for which we didn't plan at all. Those that require a quick stop to gather local produce or those that beckon us to just sit a while in a tiny city park in some tiny city.

The wheels keep on turning and Matt's story keeps on getting told as we come ever nearer to the end of YEAR 1. I mentioned earlier that there were a handful of churches (four to be exact) that God brought to us early in the Journey. We would rely on them as prayer partners and test audiences!

One of those churches is a small group of believers that worship in a beautiful windowed chapel that sits majestically on a mountainside overlooking a picturesque valley in northwest Arkansas. Congregants in this church readily offer stories of deer walking by the windows and eagles flying overhead during worship services.   Poor folks. Must be a struggle to have to worship in a place like that.

At least they also have stories to tell about finding themselves stranded at their Church during a freak snowstorm, rummaging through church kitchen cabinets for lunch while waiting for local firefighters to rescue them. There's a measure of justice in that for sure.

We first told Matt's story here on Valentines Day weekend just before our March 6 launch date. All of us experienced an amazing presence of the Holy Spirit that morning. This was a tremendous encouragement to us, since in a way; this was our "maiden voyage". We had told the story three times before, but always to people we knew, and who knew us. This "Arkansas experiment" however, would be different. I didn't know them, and they didn't know me.

Well, there actually was one man I knew.

The Pastor. And that was why we were there in the first place. I had served with him on a Church staff years earlier. When I called him and asked him if I could come to tell Matt's story, he was willing to take a risk. He said yes! This past Sunday, on our last out of town weekend (and the end of our "North of the Red River" tour) the wheels stopped rolling and we found ourselves once again in this beautiful chapel.

This time would be different. It was a chance to share our first year's experiences with these people who had committed to pray with us. Once again, I believe it is safe to say we all enjoyed an amazing presence of the Holy Spirit.

I had my thoughts for that morning decided upon until right before services would begin. My friend who

Pastors this Church is a counselor. Not just the "good friend" kind or even the "pastor" kind, but the licensed kind. His first name is Dr.

He has an interesting way about him. He can take a normal conversation, like one about football or the weather, and take it to a much deeper level well before I even know it's happening. It's kind of like watching an old WW2 movie about submarines, except no one ever warns you with an obnoxious horn and by yelling "Dive, Dive!".

This Pastor's gifts and incredible insight can produce thought provoking, soul-searching questions that "normal" people like me never see coming. Such was the case last Sunday morning right before worship was to begin.

"What do you think", he began, "is the one thing that surprised you the most during your first year? The one thing you didn't expect to happen."

Before I could help myself, I started digging deep for the answer and then I began talking. This answer wasn't hard to find, I had been wrestling with a thought for several weeks and his question seemed to be the outlet that I needed to put it into words. The answer became the theme of my message only a few minutes later.

Based on the response from our "maiden voyage" at this church back in February, we set out on our "Journey of a lifetime" full of hope. Shaunda and I now fully expected the services to be moving and potentially life changing to anyone who had traveled down our road, the loss of a child. We both hoped (and prayed) that others would be moved as well, but I think we both had little expectation.

But that was not the way it was to be. We soon noticed that every time we told Matt's story, the impact although similar, had unique characteristics. We certainly have ministered to dozens who have lost children, but also to others who have lost parents. Some have shared stories with us of their wayward children. Still others walk up after the event to talk about divorce. Yet others talk about financial difficulty and even alcoholism or family violence. Why, at one church, several young men approached me as a group to have a rather lengthy discussion about facing life's struggles at you grow older.

While travelling down America's highways between these events, Shaunda and I have found ourselves trying to determine what in the world was going on. Why was the impact of Matt's story being painted with such a broad stroke? This, it would seem, was my biggest, unexpected surprise of the year.

Shaunda, functioning as tech director for the LIVE WORSHIP EVENT is most often at the back of the rooms we play. Here she has a much better view of what is really going on than do I from the piano looking out.

"What part of the GREATER JOURNEY LIVE WORSHIP EVENT" I asked her "is really connecting?" I was expecting a response that pointed to a certain song or specific aspect of Matt's story. Her response however, truly shocked me.

There is a portion in TEARS IN A BOTTLE that is included in the LIVE WORSHIP EVENT where I talk about some of the interesting things I have had the opportunity to experience in my life. After listing several of these, I then talk about my "First Time Through the Cornfield" when it "all came crashing down around me".

"That's the part," Shaunda continued with confidence. "That's when people in these churches quit looking at you like some preacher who just walked in the door and start looking at you like you might really be one of them, someone who has experienced genuine failure in their life."

Two thirds of the way into the event we very plainly talk about Matt's death, just as I do in TEARS IN A BOTTLE. We then share in a time of intimate worship where as a group, we put into practice the concept of worshipping in the darkness as well as worshipping in the light. This is a time in the event that is not necessarily conducive to worship on first glance. The lesson here is that we worship God even when our emotions or life circumstances may not particularly line up. I learned that from Matt.

Somewhere during this first year, I finally realized that at this point in the event is where all of our individual Journeys find common ground. Whether we arrive at this intersection through the loss of a child, the loss of a spouse, the loss of a fortune, the loss of....

You get the idea, right? Our Journeys come together when we talk about loss. And therein lies the key. Although we tell Matt's story in detail, The LIVE WORSHIP EVENT is not really about cancer and death. It is more accurately about loss and hope.

The last third of Matt's story talks about our great hope as believers in Jesus. When our lives come crashing down all around us, we find hope in the reality that God can put all the broken pieces back together. When we must deal with the reality that the face of someone who is very important to us will never be seen again in this world, we find hope in realizing that it assuredly will be seen in the next.

If I believed today that my son was under six feet of dirt, I'm not sure where I would be today; but I know I wouldn't be travelling around our nation celebrating Matt's life and God's grace. Yet I find great hope this very moment in knowing without question that Matt now lives in a place where there is no more pain, no more heartache, no more tears... and no more cancer.

I guess Mr. Gaither said a mouthful when so many yeas ago he penned the lyric "Because He lives, I can face tomorrow". When we lose a loved one to an untimely death, we find hope in realizing that there is a better place for those who know Jesus.

Just don't miss the truly important words in that last sentence... those who know Jesus.

I won't ask you whether you have experienced loss. You most assuredly have, or most assuredly you soon will. This world system seems to find its very foundation in loss. The real question here is "where does your hope find its foundation?"

THE GREATER JOURNEY...

Ever see a house with an unstable foundation? You can count on cracks in the sheetrock and doors and windows that stick. If it gets bad enough, pipes will break along with a myriad of other problems. Ever try to sell a house with a bad foundation. Now there's a real problem. You may even find that your life savings is invested in a piece of real estate worth nearly nothing.

Now read Matthew 7:24-27

Take a couple moments and consider the importance of having the proper foundation for your life.

According to the verses you just read, what is that proper foundation?

CHAPTER 23
What's In A Name?

KNIGHTsong Enterprises… so where does that name come from anyway?

KNIGHTsong Enterprises has been around for a long time. You can find the logo on CD projects, old cassette projects, and even older eight track projects (Yes, "eight track". Look it up or ask someone over forty). You can find the logo on most everything I have done musically for the past thirty-five or so years. It is simply my name, Joe KNIGHT, with the suffix "SONG" identifying the endeavors as music related.

KNIGHTsong Enterprises is a registered DBA used for my musical ventures through the years. It has been attached to the many "never did much" projects and the few that "made a couple, though very small waves". It was the business name behind everything from my hand in producing and participating in my "Branson show" days to "Concept One Recording". Ever hear of "Concept One Recording"? I didn't think so. It was one of those "many"!

When I released TEARS IN A BOTTLE and later when I launched the TEARS IN A BOTTLE STUDY GUIDE and THE GREATER JOURNEY, LIVE WORSHIP

EVENT, I tagged them with the KNIGHTsong Enterprises logo. You can find it on the book and the Study Guide as well as all over the videos that play at the Live Worship Event. It was originally on our website and there was even a FaceBook page of the same name.

All well and good you might say, yet shortly after we headed out last March (2016) on YEAR 1 of this "Journey of a Lifetime" I really sensed that God was dealing with me about the "KNIGHTsong Enterprises" name. According to Webster's online dictionary the word "enterprise" is used to denote "a project or activity…that is often difficult". That fits. No problem there. It also intimates the "ability or desire to do dangerous or difficult things or to solve problems in new ways". I like that too.

There is however, another component to the definition. It seems that the word "enterprise" infers a specific economic component. It denotes a "business organization". Therein lies the source of my internal tension. While there may not be anything inherently wrong with me having a small business for distributing books or CD's, and it is certainly appropriate when producing music shows, it became painfully clear that it is to me wrong to have an "economic angle" of any kind to the telling of Matt's story.

Now please don't misunderstand me in any way. We are not taking this Journey to make money at all. Shaunda spent many years of her life involved in finances, first for a couple local Texas school districts and later for our Church. When Shaunda and I began talking seriously about setting off on this "Journey Of A

Lifetime", we came to believe at the outset that the possibility of receiving enough in offerings to cover our expenses would be highly unlikely. Forget about any salary at all.

Looking back from today's vantage point, two tours later, we were certainly correct in our initial conclusion. Fuel, daily living expenses and on and on and on requires a financial baseline that could never be sustained by the telling our story "anytime, anywhere", yet that is exactly what we feel called to do. What I am telling you is no surprise to many. We knew all of these factors from the initial planning stages and communicated these facts readily before we ever began.

Early on, with a little elementary school math we arrived at a dollar figure that would subsidize and reasonably assure a stress free two-year run at this "Journey of a Lifetime". With insight that no schooling could provide, we designed a plan that at least had a chance at reaching that "magic number" of reserve funds over the two-year period preceding our launch date.

With that the Journey really began. We sold our home and furnishings, purchased "The Virge" (our 5th wheel, lovingly named after Matt as you recall) and learned exactly what it meant to live in an RV during that first freezing winter. We learned answers for questions like "Who needs a shower every day any way?" and "Exactly how many space heaters will run on 50 amps?" We also implemented dozens of other cost cutting measures.

Please don't misunderstand the preceding paragraph. Don't perceive it as complaining. It is anything but that. It was a much-needed adventure for me! The process was great fun and a great precursor to an even greater adventure (so, how many times can one use the word "great" in one sentence?).

I also wouldn't trade those two prepatory years. I believe Shaunda and I got closer in spiritual purpose and emotional oneness as we got closer in physical confine; much closer as a matter of fact. Do you have any idea how small 396 square feet is? Ask me, or better yet, ask Shaunda. We discovered, as well, how freeing it is to live without so many of the "things" we found out we never really needed anyway.

As we worked the plan, made every acquisition for our future Journey and worked through every challenge, I discovered that I was learning how to dream all over again. The process may have taken two years, yet it seemed that somehow at the end I was younger by many times the two years I invested. I can honestly say that I would gladly repeat those two years with it's challenges even if the Journey never came to be at all. It meant that much to me.

With many other "budget adjustments" and a ton of prayer we reached our financial goal before the March 6, 2016 launch date. Apparently it was really going to happen; and "happen" it did. The way God has moved to this point has been indescribable at best.

Our commitment to this Journey has been to tell our story "anytime, anywhere". I do not believe that hurting people are only in Churches of certain size or of certain financial standing. I likewise do not believe that the lessons God taught me that are recorded in TEARS IN A BOTTLE would be of advantage only to people who have the financial means to purchase it.

We determined from the beginning that none of these factors would be a consideration in scheduling. Early in the Journey we ran into a recurring process that brought about a level of uncomfortability for us from the outset. That process? Making change at our book table. Somehow we both seemed to feel somewhat like "moneychangers" dealing in cash instead of ministers dealing in hope.

Please don't misunderstand what I am telling you now. I am not saying that I am better than anyone else. I am not saying that I have discovered the "right" thing to do, and that everyone else is doing it "wrong". I am not saying that we were "wrong" to begin with. I'm not even saying that what we are doing is smart. I am merely sharing with you this "Journey of a Lifetime", as it happens.

Enter into this equation the "Men of Monday Morning". These are four men of similar age and life stage to me. I have shared countless hours of early Monday morning prayer and bible study over a period of a few years, as well as more than a few breakfasts.

Don't misunderstand this either; this is not an instance of a staff Pastor pouring himself into four men. It is rather five men pouring themselves into each other. These are the men with whom I have a level of relationship shared only by those who have common purpose and shared experiences, and a few facts better not shared outside of the room we met in. We began long before the Journey was even conceived, and it is this group that beta tested the TEARS IN A BOTTLE STUDY GUIDE.

The week before the Journey began, our wives joined the five of us for a wonderful "going away" dinner. At the end of the evening following a large amount of awesome food and even a few tears, we all joined hands for a "commissioning prayer" of sorts. At the conclusion they proposed to me an idea; the same idea that was strongly suggested by another man several months earlier.

Years ago a gentleman approached me after the morning worship with a strange introductory line. "Seems we have something in common," he said. "I lost my son on March 15th as well". This person is a retired businessman and former mayor of a good sized city on the West Coast. That first morning's conversation led to a friendship. The friendship led to mentorship. When I began talking about this unique Journey, I sought business advice from him early on. He had suggested the same idea.

Add to these facts, suggestions and difficulties, a glaring reality. I genuinely believe that I have been called to be a Pastor. True, I have written a book and have two in the process, but I have no desire to be considered an author. I have several CD and DVD projects (and more in the works), but I have no desire to be considered a recording artist. Good thing on both accounts. I'm not certain I possess the giftedness for either. I still however, possess a singular desire to be what I am; a Pastor.

As of this writing, I still have no vision for this ministry past the initial two years. David, speaking to God, said in Psalm 119:105 that "Your word is a lamp for my feet, a light on my path" (NIV). The psalmist teaches us here that the Word of God gives us direction, but sometimes only for the next step. This verse speaks of a journey taken at night. Why else would we need a lamp at all? The lamp held low illuminated only the immediate path to the front to protect from dangers hidden by the darkness. The emphasis on "feet" and "path" teaches us that the light of God's direction sometimes only provides vision for one phase of a Journey; only the next step if you will. The remainder of the Journey is there as certain as if we could see it clearly. It's just that Journey must be taken by faith just as the light illumines only the next step.

It is here that I still find myself. I have no hint yet what God holds for our future direction at the end of this two-year "Journey of a Lifetime". With the advice of friends firmly seated in my decision making process, I do however want to be completely equipped for whatever may come.

So what does this all mean? KNIGHTsong Enterprises, take a back seat. Let me introduce you to KNIGHTsong Ministries.

Right or wrong, smart or not so smart, we have completely rethought our product table over the past months. We no longer "sell" anything. A small, unobtrusive square black box sits at a location provided by each church. Most of the time we are not even in the vicinity. (I know, I know. Remember I've been a cop as well. This goes against everything I have learned to dislike about human nature). I encourage those who truly believe they would benefit from any product we offer to make a donation at whatever level they see fit. I cannot tell you for sure that we are not being taken advantage of. I *can* tell you two other things for sure though. I believe that some give a large amount, yet walk away with a bargain and that others place far less in the box, and yet have given much more. Besides, this way we never have to make change!

If there was any doubt that this was what God wanted us to do, it cowered its ugly head and slithered out the door a few Sundays ago. I met a young lady who was raising a blended family of children of varied ages, nine in total (Yes, NINE!). Even after I shared with the congregation that morning and reiterated personally to her after the service that she need not give anything, she instead shared a rather strong response. "No way. It's just that I don't have much money". She then dropped a small amount in the square black box as she told me that her husband recently passed away leaving her with those nine children to raise by herself. He passed away within a few weeks of when our March Journey began.

I don't know how much she gave. I would never share the exact amount if I knew. I wouldn't have ever known she gave anything had I not been standing right there on this particular occasion. I do know that it was a small amount. I would say however, that if most of you reading this had misplaced this same amount, I doubt you would have wasted much time searching for it. I would also submit that from a biblical perspective she likely gave more for her book than anyone else on this tour.

So... I am supposed to put a price tag on this incredible message of hope? God forbid. I wonder if this lady has any idea how important her gift really was to me.

The advice from my retired mayor mentor all those months earlier? Establish a 501(c)3 not for profit ministry organization. "There are others who will want to take this Journey with you, but they can never leave home".

The idea the "Men of Monday Morning" presented at our going away party? The same. Their concept however, was less like advice and more like a well thought out plan. "We think you should establish 501(c)3, and furthermore, we think that we should be your board".

I argued that I already had the money to fund this two-year Journey. The response: Maybe God wants to use that money for a year three or beyond. And besides, are you required to spend it all?

I argued that I wanted to do this and not "take" from anyone else. The response: What if God wants us, and others like us, to help you and you won't let us?

I argued that I couldn't take money from God's people to pay for books and fuel, let alone for food and shelter. The response: How is that different from what you have been doing as a Church Pastor for the past 35 years?

I argued that although true, it just feels different without a Church in between. The response: That's what we will do. We will be that organization and accountability in-between.

Fast forward several months and KNGHTsong Ministries is now organized and is a fully approved and recognized 501(c)3 organization. The board is comprised of four men of good standing, reputable and honest. Shaunda brings her vast experience to keep up with the appropriate government and associated paperwork as any gifts are now fully tax deductible.

This is not an excuse to raise funds; it is merely an association put in place in the event others desire to share financially with this ministry. It is a mechanism to further this ministry past the two years should God so lead. To date I have done my best to graciously decline funding offered by several individuals. Three Pastors wanting to know if we were willing to be considered as a monthly supported ministry similar to a Missionary have also approached me. This new association satisfies all the legal obligations to make both avenues available.

This is not to be perceived as a commitment to continue past year two, or even an attempt to intimate that there are currently any plans for the future. At present, I am merely taking small steps while looking only to the light that is displayed on the pathway directly ahead. It is a light that illuminates only the place where my foot will land next. So in the meantime, I'm reworking all the avenues possible to communicate a "ministry" emphasis instead of an "enterprise" emphasis. And the best part of it for me?

This identifies me not as a singer/songwriter, or author/consultant, orn police officer/whatever, but rather as a Pastor.

And for the record, I love it, every moment of it. I do not know what the future holds, but for now I am enjoying every day and every new adventure, and even the unpredictability it brings. And to be quite honest, I wonder how young I might become in a few more years.

Now, how about a note from my friend...

Should you like to support this ministry financially, you can do so by sending your tax-deductible gifts to:

KNIGHTSONG Ministries
PO Box 647
Commerce, TX   75429

Russell Armstrong for The KNIGHTSONG MINISTRIES Board

CHAPTER 24
Lessons In The Sand

While working on this book I have purposely avoided current events for a couple of reasons. Current events are by their very nature, current. As such, any comments concerning these types of things would likely lose any applicability to future readers, as the vast majority of today's current events will soon become tomorrow's forgotten history.

Equally, if not more importantly, is the reality that different people view current events through drastically different "eyes", or life experiences if you will. It is an undisputed fact that two persons from differing backgrounds can consider identical facts and reach diametrically opposing conclusions. It is also a fact that in our nation today we have never experienced a time when current events are interpreted from such opposing narratives. As such, writing about any polarizing topic is running the risk of hitting one of those opposing narratives head on.

Even with these factors considered, I will assume the risks and venture into the area of current events... current to our Fall 2016 United States that is.

This "Journey of a Lifetime" has afforded me many amazing opportunities to enjoy some of the incredible historical locations our country has to offer. This week I had the honor (I chose that word intentionally) to spend a day at the World War II museum in New Orleans, Louisiana. This world-class museum is a historically accurate time capsule of the singular greatest global struggle our world has ever known, at least till now.

I have always considered myself a minor student of World War II. My fascination began in Junior High school where nearly every English paper I wrote was themed around a major World War II event beginning with the Battle of Midway. I continued my interest into adulthood having read many books, visited every associated location I have come across here in the states. I have also watched every John Wayne Movie concerning the subject. (That last part was intended as a bit of comic relief. You may need it in a minute.)

In mostly chronological order this museum tells the story of the major events of this global struggle along with many other events I had never heard of. This incredible journey through time also enlightens visitors with facts and stories about the major leaders on all sides of this conflict. These are leaders with names like Ike, Patton, Stalin, Churchill and Tojo. It also goes to even greater lengths to introduce you to dozens of individual soldiers whose names are relatively unknown and whose stories have been mostly forgotten and swept away by the ever-changing sands of time. They had names like Bill, John and Gary.
Some of these were professional soldiers. Most were citizen soldiers. These "citizen soldiers" were normal

people who were truck drivers delivering vegetables one day, and soldiers charging a machine gun emplacement the next. Some came home when they completed final missions only to find themselves forever changed. Many completed their final mission and never came home at all.

The experience that seemed the most profound to me today was an exhibit in the section of the museum dedicated to Operation Overlord; the D-Day landings in Normandy, more specifically at Omaha beach. Now this amphibious operation was by no means the only offensive of it's type in World War II, but certainly is the best known. As a side note, I'm not sure why it is not mandatory for every public school student to read a Stephen Ambrose work and "With The Old Breed" by Eugene Sledge. Perhaps if they did, this chapter would not need to be written at all. And it really shouldn't have to be.

The location that I found particularly engaging was centered on a simple glass display case some five or six feet in width. Nearby were two tattered American flags displayed vertically, also preserved in glass cases. Above was a very limited amount of text. The words were a reprint of a portion of a news story written by the iconic World War II war correspondent Ernie Pyle. Pyle poignantly described with his words the emotion he felt as he returned to Omaha beach late on the afternoon of June 6. Published on June 17, 1944 in the Los Angeles Times, here are some of those words...

"Here are socks and shoe polish, sewing kits, diaries, Bibles and hand grenades.... Here are toothbrushes

and razors, and snapshots of families back home staring up at you from the sand."

The brutal, bloody battle fought on this few yards of beach began at dawn. It was one of extraordinary bravery and unspeakable sacrifice. It was here that Rommel's beach defenses and concentrated firepower came the closest to driving the Allied soldiers back into the English Channel.

The planning and training for the very moment of invasion, H-hour, had been underway in the lives of most of these former "truck drivers" for two years. This patch of sandy beach was the exact place where hundreds of them fell lifeless into the water, cut down by vicious direct and enfilading fire at the very moment the ramp on the front of their landing craft crashed into the surf.

Late that same afternoon of June 6, 1944, a near miracle beach breakout was accomplished with great cost. It was carried out mostly by infantry without the benefit of command staff, most of whom had also perished in similar numbers earlier in the morning.

It was after this breakout that Ernie returned to the beach. Here is where he described the items he saw. Each item told a story. Each helmet, each bible, every personal effect, and every picture.

Then I glanced down into the display case below the words and looked directly at a faded photograph lying on a bed of sand. The smartly dressed, smiling young lady in the photo was arm in arm with the equally handsome young man in uniform. He was likewise smiling. They both seemed so full of life. He was also numbered among those who would never go home again. As you read this today his life's blood is forever mingled with the waters of the English Channel.

I then looked for a very long time at the tattered American flags.

My first response to that flag was to take a knee.

You see, I have something to protest as well. I could take this opportunity to make my statement and express my negative opinions about America. You see; I too am disappointed about what our nation has become.

I could have shouted out loud that I find myself ashamed when I acknowledge the fact that the number of innocent babies sacrificed on the altar of convenience is greater than the number of American young men and women forever lost in all of America's wars. I am appalled when people of political influence commit grievous offenses and engage in flagrant, obvious cover-ups, and then carry on as if they have done nothing wrong.

Instead, I held my words. In the presence of such sacrifice is not the place to express any opinion of mine regardless of how righteous. Now to be completely honest, when I stared at that faded, tattered flag this week, I really didn't feel as if I should take a knee. I actually felt I should take both knees, and then bow my head and thank God for those who bought for us, with their own blood, the very freedom to do disgusting, disrespectful things.

Taking a knee during the national anthem at a football game is highly disrespectful to say the least. But athletes have the right to be disrespectful. We all do for that matter. When I was in junior high school the American Flag was routinely burned, urinated on and used to patch holes on the seats of our blue jeans. The Supreme Court determined that we had the right to do that too.

It's probably best though, that we don't get angry with those who exercise their rights in an effort to bring attention to their ill-conceived conclusions that are based on their particular narrative, no matter how flawed that narrative may be. We might instead extend pity to them for possessing such an incomplete appreciation of the sacrifice that secured them that right. And whatever you do, don't react to them. I fear that if we do, we are giving them exactly what they want.

Rather, let's pray for them. Pray that they will learn to respect the sacrifice of so many that gives them the right to choose in the first place.

Pray they decide to worry less about their right and simply decide to do the right thing... if not for themselves, how about for the man in the picture?

Let's pray that regardless of their age, they will one day grow up and realize that just because an American has the right to do something, does not make it right to do.

THE GREATER JOURNEY...

John 15:13
Greater love has no one than this: to lay down one's life for one's friends.

Let's take a few moments just to consider a scenario. Imagine for a moment that the young man whose picture I described was somehow miraculously transported to the very spot where you are right now reading these words.

What would you say to him?
How would you thank him for his sacrifice?
How would you express your gratitude?

Now imagine for a moment that in a single instant you were transported into the presence of Jesus Christ Himself. Consider the same three questions, and then realize one absolute fact.

The first scenario could never happen. The second scenario cannot be avoided.

CHAPTER 25
Thanksgiving

 YEAR ONE has worked it's way around the calendar to Thanksgiving, and I have so much to be thankful for. This first year of our JOURNEY OF A LIFETIME has been truly amazing. I have been told that sometimes what I share should be rated PT; possible tears.

Yet I do not share to make you cry, or to bring about any emotional response at all for that matter. I share with the prayer that you sense the deeper message and *choose* right now that you will make every moment count this Thanksgiving.

> *Choose*... to not share harsh words with anyone around you, even if the stress of the Holidays is upon you.

> *Choose*... to spend time with your family, even if it means yielding the ultimate power of the television remote.

Choose... to be thankful in all things, even if all things are not exactly as you would like them to be.

This Thanksgiving day will find Poppi seated at the dining room table, perhaps even next to the most precious Granddaughter in the world. I might even be close to my new Grandson as his wide eyes give light to his very first Thanksgiving. When we join hands around the table, it will be with family; parents, a daughter, a son-in-law, a son and friends. When I squeeze my right hand as we say our Thanksgiving prayers, the love of my life; the one who I have sat right beside as we travelled all across the United States this year, will squeeze back with her left hand. During the day, the telephone will melt away the miles as we reconnect with friends and family.

Or perhaps none of this will happen at all.

What if the time allotted for my life reaches an unexpected conclusion? What if I close my eyes tonight and never wake up at all? What if the Archangel gives his final shout?

Then I will sit at another table this Thanksgiving, perhaps even next to Matt. I might even be close to my parents with whom I have not enjoyed a Thanksgiving meal for many years. When we join hands around the table it would also be with family; parents, a son and more friends than I could name. Who knows? When I squeeze my right hand as we say our Thanksgiving prayers, what if I found that the one who has been right beside me as I travelled all through this life was squeezing back with His left hand?

It is with that desire that we are presented with the challenge to never take one moment of life for granted. One thing is for certain... we may never pass this way again. What a tremendous Thanksgiving lesson of hope.

THE GREATER JOURNEY...

Read 1 Thessalonians 5:18, then consider this two-part challenge.

FIRST...
Make a list of everything you can think of that you are thankful for. Job, family, church, home, salvation, everything.

SECOND...
Start at your list from the top and make a concerted effort to say thank you to everyone who made these things possible.

Today might just feel like Thanksgiving regardless of the date.

CHAPTER 26
Happy Endings

Nine straight weekends of music and telling Matt's story have delivered us to a place where we can catch a breath and enjoy some family time. I know that time is relative to the event (seems I heard that one somewhere). As such, I'm good with it slowing down a bit.

Christmas is right around the corner and "The Virge" is sharing in the festivities. I am writing this flanked by a single strand of lighted garland and a three-foot Christmas tree bedecked with literally tens of lights and a dozen or so ornaments (not a lot of space you know).   And then a mere week later, it will be New Years Eve and the end of 2016.

I'm a sucker for happy endings. At this time of the year there are plenty of them to go around. Not in real life you understand, but rather on the TV in the form of sappy Holiday movies. Seems that this year those Christmas movies started their seemingly unending loop of showtimes while the outside temperature in Texas was still hovering in the upper 90's. We all realize that these movies have one common goal; to make us cry. You can count on that. As embarrassing as it is to admit, more often than not I have fallen victim to their primary intention. Like I said, I'm a sucker for happy endings.

Regardless of the time period of the movie, the actors involved or the plot, they all have several things in common. The leading ladies are all thin, unrealistically thin. They always have beautifully curled hair and flawless makeup regardless of the time of day, including when they first get out of bed in the morning. I'm not certain what gifts the leading men in these mostly "made for TV" movies really get for Christmas, but apparently they don't include a razor. It's difficult to find a clean-shaven face among them.

Here are a few other things you can count on. There are always children involved, and they are all too cute, too wonderful and too, well… just too everything. They nearly always are missing a father whether by divorce or death. Don't worry though. The unshaven hero will soon arrive and affect an epic rescue.

These movies have other characters in common as well. They are sometimes strangers who all too often turn out to be long lost relatives. Sometimes they are relatives who, at first, act more like strangers. Often they are covert angels. Similar Christmas themes and Christmas scenes randomly surface as well.

There are always "unspoken truths" in play. They leave us just wishing that "he would just tell her" or "she would linger a moment longer" in the coffee shop (or the donut shop, or the restaurant or the hardware store). In this way they could accidentally meet yet again. "He" is often the secret admirer; "she" is the lost and lonely soul whose every need could be met in a whirlwind moment, or perhaps not. They might actually miss their one great opportunity in life and their Christmases will be a total flop. Cue the dramatic music.

As always, spare yourself any unnecessary concern. The needle and thread events that are randomly weaving their way through the fabric of the plot guarantee a tidy ending. Here all these seemingly unrelated pieces will magically come together. Eighty-three minutes of "stuff", and seven minutes of happy endings. (Well, how about that. Come to think of it, they really all have the same basic plot as well.)

You are guaranteed a few important events in the final seven minutes of the movie. The guy will get the girl, or the girl will get the guy depending on your perspective. The children will get a family along with all the Christmas gifts they really wanted, but Mom could not afford. The adults will buy the lodge or turn down the awesome job they were just offered to remain in their hometown and run the family business. AND FINALLY... wait for it... it will start to snow.

Take this Holiday mixture, fold in a few Christmas carols and add a pinch of humor. Top it with a starry night highlighted by one special star and you will experience the guaranteed sure thing; a happy ending. So hide the remote and bring on the Kleenex. Like I said, I'm a sucker for happy endings.

The only problem is that real life is not at all like the movies. We live in a fallen world where good is often called evil, and evil is lauded as good. Moms don't always love their children and wayward Dads seldom come home. Far too often the reason there is no money for the gifts is that Dad drank it up or Mom traded it for a small bag of a white powdery substance on the wrong side of town near the intersection of hapless road and hopeless avenue.

Even at this happiest of all happy times of the year, many families self-destruct and innocent children die of cancer. Elderly, forgotten parents welcome Christmas morning from a squeaky rocker where they sit alone in the darkness while the cold winds whistle as they work their way around windows long in need of repair. Moms fall into the arms of men who are not their husbands while husbands pass out on a stool next to a painted stranger underneath a flashing neon light.

So where are all the good times? Where is the TV romance? Where are all the happy endings? Where is the snow? Seems that while many of us enjoy our friends and family, so many others who surround us are suffering through private pain, and we are powerless to effect any real change.

Enter into the stark hopelessness of this lost world, a small baby, a baby that was born specifically to be the Savior of the world. From the humble feed trough He stretched both hands upward toward His heavenly Father until the day the Roman soldiers took them and nailed them to a cross. On that rugged, splintery wood suspended between heaven and earth He paid the price for every sin for every man and every woman ever born. When we realize the meaning of His sacrifice and find ourselves ready to bend our knee we discover life's greatest miracle. At that moment our sins and our Savior come face to face. The ensuing explosion of grace blasts our disgusting failures to a place where even God Himself can never find them. The holiness of God the Father is satisfied. We walk away clean, with a fresh start.

Many of us have been at the top of the sin chart or the bottom of the bottle and yet His grace reached us even there. Perhaps you find yourself alone in the darkness, and now you realize that you really are not alone at all. His grace reaches you there too.

And maybe, just maybe the reason it doesn't feel like you are experiencing the full "television version" of life is because you've missed one big fact. In this world we are living in those first eighty-three minutes. These are the times when life is confusing. Times when we don't linger long enough in the coffee shop; a time when the special moments are missed and the "unspoken truths" remain undiscovered, just out of our reach.

But don't give up. The "seven minutes" are just ahead. The needle and thread events that are randomly weaving their way through the fabric of our lives are actually not random at all. What's more is, that for those of us who know Christ, I can guarantee a happy ending. One day all of these seemingly unrelated pieces will gloriously come together in a place where there is no more pain, no more heartache, no more loneliness… and no more death.

But you can keep the Kleenex. At this happy ending we won't need them. My God Himself will wipe away every tear from our eyes.

THE GREATER JOURNEY...

*Hope deferred makes the heart sick, but a
longing fulfilled is a tree of life.
Proverbs 13:12*

**Far too often we mistakenly try to rationalize our
life experiences based entirely on the life that we
now experience. Considered in this way, it is
entirely possible to come to the conclusion that
our God is cruel, heartless or worse. And if this
life were all that there is, I fear that this would be
a reasonable conclusion. Try telling a young
lady who is a thirty-five year old quadriplegic to
quit being so discouraged.**

**Now consider whatever hopeless scenario you
can imagine, witnessed or experienced and
factor in eternity.**

*I consider that our present sufferings are not
worth comparing with the glory
that will be revealed in us.
Romans 8:18*

CHAPTER 27
What I Want For Christmas

Well, there it is. The theme of innumerable Holiday movies and no doubt the topic of millions of school essays again this year. For me as a child growing up, this was a difficult dilemma. It seemed the list was nearly endless. My parents solved this problem in a way that kept me from experiencing a debilitating dose of writer's cramp. They presented me three department store Christmas catalogues and a crayon. I simply had to circle the appropriate desired treasures.

It was many years later that I realized that the nature of my Father's seasonal employment and the fact that these catalogues had corresponding charge cards were the fuel that powered their plan. This is not a method that I would ever recommend, but from where I sit today looking back, I see only their sacrifice. Maybe now it makes sense why when Christmas morning finally arrived, it seemed that Santa brought me so many gifts, while bringing my parents so few, and sometimes none at all.

Thanks Mom and Dad. Why is it that it sometimes seems to take so many years to realize how grateful we should have been?

As the years have flown by, my "wish list" has changed drastically. It has continually become smaller. Please don't misunderstand; it's not that I have so much. As a matter of fact, I have less "stuff" this year than I have had at any Christmas in recent memory. It's just that I have everything I need. The more I try to follow Christ, the less I find that I need "stuff".

I don't want this to come across as arrogant piety in any way. Just consider this spiritual principle. There is absolutely nothing wrong with having "stuff", but there is everything wrong with needing it. If you are not attached to your possessions emotionally, you will not miss them if you have to leave them behind. Consider this: one way or another, you will one day leave them all behind. God never said we couldn't enjoy what we have, He just wants "what we have" to remain in its proper perspective.

So what do I want for Christmas? It's not in any printed department store catalogue or on any website. You won't see it advertised between mindless television shows on child specific channels. You won't even find it on any shelf at your favorite discount department store. Actually, I can tell you that what I want is something I have never seen, although I have sensed its presence twice before in my life, and neither instance shared the calendar with any particular Holiday.

Many years ago as a young man, I had the privilege to travel to many of our United States as part of a southern Gospel quartet. "Southern Gospel" someone just exclaimed out loud. Absolutely. And what's more, at the time we did this, we were cutting edge to say the least. My Mother, perhaps one of the most overprotective moms in history, somehow consented to allowing me and several other teenagers to jump into a 35-foot diesel bus and tour the Country. Talk about an adventure.

We sang at concerts, church services and several summer church youth camps. As I recall, many of the latter were amazing experiences replete with uproarious fun and incredible worship services. We sang during the day as well as at the evening events and I often had the opportunity to speak. The remainder of the days were filled with activities where we had the chance to interact with the campers since we were really not much older than they were. This provided some great opportunities to gain credibility with those campers.

One of these summer youth camps was particularly unique. The host pastor for this event was a man with a history of being a successful teen speaker and motivator. He was also what I would have described at that time as a "health food nut". He would have rivaled Euell Gibbons. Go ahead, don't resist it. Do an Internet search. You may even find yourself shouting aloud with Solomon: "There is nothing new under the sun".

This particular youth camp experience found granola bars and fruit juice favored over candy bars and soda pop ("soda pop", I know, I'm a "Yankee"). In fact, more than "favored", they were legislated. Even the "snack shack" was stripped of all vestiges of carbonated drinks and sugar laden candy in favor of natural juices, and "candy like" bars that actually had more in common with a tree than with chocolate. Carrot sticks were offered as a lame substitute for chips.

Consider with this the fact that the sponsoring Church had undertaken a huge push for evangelism well in advance of the camp dates. This "push for evangelism" included a very successful campaign in a large neighboring city to scholarship a large contingency of inner city youngsters of varying cultural and ethnic backgrounds. These were young men and women significantly more street smart than anyone else in attendance including any adult counselor or guest musician. Seems they had been recruited with an emphasis on fun activity with precious little information shared with regard to the mandate that they would be subjected to Christian music and teaching; every day; multiple times a day.

If that is not enough of a recipe for disaster, consider that without warning they discovered they could only supplement their indescribable and entirely unexpected camp food diet with carrot sticks, apple juice and granola bars. Anybody want to go to camp?

These "visitors" seemed quite disinterested in playing softball. Opportunities for nature hikes were also less than enticing. "Medicine Ball" held little attraction. It seems like while most of the middle class "church kids" had been listening to Karen Carpenter on the radio, trying to make the cheerleading squads and keeping up their tans, the "guest kids" had been surviving on the streets of the early 1970's inner city simply trying to stay alive.

Here in this small Christian camp almost equal representatives of these two diametrically opposed cultures would clash and try to find common ground. Remember that this scenario came about by no accident at all. This crazy youth guy had planned it all well in advance. This "nut case" preacher believed that the Gospel of Jesus Christ could actually change lives and bridge social divides. All of this explains the spiritual motivation, but it sure doesn't account for the fruit juice at the snack shack. I still don't comprehend that decision. No worries. Soon we would discover a workaround.

With this strange diversity in place our drummer counted off four beats, the band entered and the vocals kicked off a rousing southern gospel tune. It became my responsibility to lead this group in worship. I may as well have been singing on the moon.

Now as for the church crowd, they were in utter shock, and they loved it. Keep in mind they spent their Sundays locked inside churches where leaders were smashing "rock music" records one Sunday and singing every verse of five hymns the next. These hymns were accompanied by piano and organ and led by a man in a white shirt and a fat tie that ended well above his belt buckle. He usually sported a pocket protector and was waving his arms in an unusual, inexplicable erratic fashion. To this "churchy" crowd our music was new, fresh and alive. It held musical nuances that were not all that different from what they were listening to on the radio, and they loved it.

The inner city crowd? They were in utter shock as well, and likely also felt that the not so gently used school bus turned church bus that delivered them only a day earlier had also accidentally landed on the moon.

We however, had a secret weapon. We brought our own candy, chips and soda pop. (i.e. soda, carbonated beverage, insert your favorite brand name here and pretend it represents all brands)

We also set out to crash into their culture.

We began our plan to combat their disinterest in innate "camp like" activities. Instead of softball, we talked. Instead of nature hikes, we walked around the campground trying to understand what their lives were all about. And I had a lot to learn. I don't know what you have heard about the early 1970's from television and movie portrayals, but in my safe northeastern Ohio suburban school, I was in class with only one guy we knew regularly smoked pot. He smelled funny and slept through the second half of our split English class, the half that was right after lunch three days a week.

These kids I was now trying to understand lived in a much less benign environment. They were living in the post 1960's inner city where the seeds of unrest were sown into their lives daily. It was time now to deploy our secret weapon.

With stealth that would surely impress the Green Berets of the day, we shared our treasure, our secret stash. Our talks were now laced with coke, not the powdery kind mind you, but rather the diet or regular kind. I actually caught one of my guys trying to sell this contraband at inflated black market prices to more than willing customers. I made him give back their money. Mix in a few hidden candy bars and bags of chips and we were in.

And the church services? They were absolute disasters. Monday, Tuesday, Wednesday and Thursday, both the days and the nights, all the same. We sang our hearts out. Other preachers and teachers spoke with passion as well. Group leaders led small groups in quiet discussion that seemed to take place in the cone of silence (so I'm in a 70's mode while writing this, big deal!). Our group sang the same songs in the same way we had done many times. I brought messages that had successfully set other teens on their ears. This time? Nothing. Nada. Just cold silence that found our musicians approaching desperation. Why desperation? Because these "kids" whose culture we were somehow trying to grasp, now had names, and faces, and stories of their own.

Very soon Saturday morning would arrive with the smell of diesel permeating the air, we would load up our A7s, hop on the bus and embrace the highway once again, and likely never see any of these souls again. But now it was Thursday night; and we seemed powerless to make any difference. It was then that one of the young "preacher boys" of the church youth group approached me with an idea.

"I'm gonna pray tonight, all night. Wanna join me?" he asked.

After another indescribably lousy supper, after the death knell of a service, after the childish games that followed the service and after lights out, we met at the flagpole.

"I'm heading out to the woods," the young man said. "I don't want anyone to hear me".
Huh? I thought. That's an easy fix. Stay here and pray quietly. That however, was not his style.

We walked down a long path and deep into the dark woods, the path illuminated only by our flashlights. I still remember how warm and humid the oppressive summer night air was. It seemed to closely mimic the heavy spirit that had overtaken the entire youth camp. Then with the stars watching down on us from above, this young man began to pray. I will never forget the first three words he yelled: "Oh God...please!".

And I do mean yelled. He literally cried out to God, as did the other counselors who joined us. There were no leaders here, just a group of young men. And we prayed.

We then changed locations to where we could see each dormitory where the campers were housed. With outstretched hands, the names of the campers were spoken out loud along with their needs, and their stories. Wow, it seemed that "churchy" suburban campers have needs too. Many of their lives were broken. The major difference was that their drama tended to play out quietly behind closed doors. Doors that allowed a facade to be perpetrated while moms and dads quietly tried to come to grips with financial issues and failed marriages. Another difference was that these families, like so many today, tended to mask their pain with expensive wine and prescription drugs, instead of the illegal substitutions for both.

The prayer session moved to the chapel; down each row stopping at every seat. Every teenager that anyone in the prayer cadre could think of was prayed for by name. Those who couldn't be named were prayed for by description. "God, please save the crusty, edgy kid from the streets; the one who sits here every night in the dirty sleeveless t-shirt."

"God, please! This young man that will sit here; he has worn the same shirt every night. He doesn't even have money for snacks, (I mean granola.) He doesn't know you God. Please don't let him spend eternity in hell".

We couldn't personally do anything about the spiritual need, that was between him and God. Little did anyone know that he didn't need any money for snacks. He hated fruit juice. But no fear, he had the hook up for the black market carbonated beverages.

On and on it went. All night. Literally. It continued until before we knew it the sun began peeking through the trees. I returned to our cabin, took a quick shower, skipped breakfast and literally ran into the chapel barely in time for morning worship.

And nothing special happened.

It was just like all the other services. Quiet. Lonely. Disjointed, Disappointing. Yet we continued to pray, all day long.

The hours passed uneventfully. It finally came time for the closing service. We were to sing, I was to speak. Everyone gathered as usual. And that was the last "usual" thing that would happen.

That night we sang only two songs as I recall. The first an up-tempo opener, the second, a song I had recently written. It is a very simple VCVC tune. Verse one deals plainly with Christ's sacrifice on the cross, followed by a four line chorus that in simple words reminds us that He never gave up on us. Verse two deals with our failure to fully appreciate what that sacrifice represents, and the reality that, despite our failures and the fact that we often give up on Him, He never once gave up on us.

In between the two verses I would speak plainly about the horrific nature of the crucifixion, and the fact that Christ chose the cross. I stressed the reality that Christ did not die from crucifixion, nor did he die when the soldier violently shoved the spear into his side. As a matter of fact, He did not die by man's hand at all. He was God.

"No man takes my life from me" Christ Himself proclaimed. "I lay it down".

Jesus was man *and* God. You can't kill God. Jesus *chose* to lay down His life.

And Jesus had done nothing wrong, not ever. He didn't sin. He did not deserve what was happening to Him, yet because He loved us so much and didn't want us to live and die in abject hopelessness, so He provided a pathway to hope, not only for this life, but also for the life yet to come.

The message that night was simple, the music even simpler. Yet light bulbs came on all over the room. It was soon evident that it is of little difference where or how your hopelessness plays out. It may manifest itself on the mean streets where illegal drugs flourish amidst rampant unemployment and unabashed hatred. A place where "f-bombs" are commonplace and anarchy lurks around every corner. It also may make its unwelcome appearance in one of three beautifully appointed bedrooms where a precious teenage girl buries her face in a pillow while her world implodes. Her quiet sobs cannot drown out the chaos in her heart as mom and dad exchange barbed words that ultimately end with "That's it, we're through".

Hopelessness makes its presence known everywhere. Oddly enough, it is only when we truly comprehend our hopeless state without Christ that we can truly embrace the hope we find in His sacrifice.

That's about all there was to the service that night; a service that lasted for four hours, yes FOUR hours. No more special songs, no formal sermon. Just more than three and one half hours of an invitation that included every worship song and hymn I knew.

Teenagers of all colors, shapes and sizes came forward in waves. Some waited patiently for nearly an hour just for their turn to have someone pick up a Bible and show them how to receive Christ. Some counselors and adult workers trusted Christ too. Others came and made decisions and choices to more genuinely follow Christ. Still others made decisions to surrender their lives for vocational ministry. Some did all three.

I would venture that everyone in the room came forward that night at one time or another, most of them more that once. Even that crusty, edgy kid from the streets; the one in the dirty sleeveless t-shirt.

I didn't sleep the night before this service and I don't think I really slept for the next few nights either. The next day, now safely deposited back in our bus, even the hum of the tires and the sound of the interstate rushing by couldn't sing its usual lullaby. I just stared at the bottom of the bunk above me through worshipping tears.

I learned so much that week. I knew that planning and preparation was a vital part of revival. I learned that programs, plans or the latest strategy by themselves are guaranteed to be a failure in God's eyes. Genuine success is totally dependent upon the presence and power of His Spirit. I learned that relationship is often the key to influence. I learned that God can work just fine in what we perceive to be an environment of unholy silence. I mostly learned how to pray.

Today I realize that the campers were not the only impressionable young people in attendance that hot, humid summer week now more than forty years in my past.

At Christmas this year I wouldn't mind opening a Fort Apache play set, a Jungle Jim safari kit or even a chemistry set, provided they matched their catalogue picture that I carefully circled. I wouldn't even mind a few more gift cards! (We saved ours for three years before beginning our Journey of a Lifetime so we could use them on the road.) It's just that with the exception of one other time, and that is a story for another day, I never experienced that type of revival again. But I really do want to.

Its what I really want for Christmas.

THE GREATER JOURNEY...

What is the best Christmas gift you ever received? You know, that gift that you think of nearly every Holiday season when you're feeling like a child.

Have you ever said "Thank you?"

Could you say "thank you" right now? You could send a text or make a phone call. You could write them a letter, even if they have long since left this world.

In that same spirit of gratitude, how long has it been since you made the opportunity to say "thank you" to the One who gave you the greatest gift of all?

Consider the lesson we can learn from the following passage:

Luke 17:12-19

If you were Jesus, how would you feel about the nine lepers who did not return? How would you feel about the one who did?

What kind of a person do you want to be? It could be that the simple act of remembering Christ's sacrifice might just be the beginning of a revival in your heart.

1 Peter 1:5-9

Part 4
GO *(south)* WEST
(not so) YOUNG MAN

CHAPTER 28
Go (South)West (Not So)Young Man

Hope you're in a forgiving mood since I began this chapter by unapologetically butchering a rather famous Horace Greeley quote. It's just that it seemed to allow me to put a label on this first tour of YEAR 2. And speaking of YEAR 2 and "direction", seems as well that this is the perfect time to remind all of us what this "Journey of a Lifetime" is all about. Wow, a butchered quote followed immediately by a vague, uncomfortable segue. This ought to be fun!

As I stated a little over a year ago (or in some cases several chapters ago) the title JOURNEY OF A LIFETIME has an intended double meaning. First off, I have invested the majority of my life as a Pastor. There is no complaint at all here, but as such that choice pretty well guaranteed that I would not retire with a healthy pension or bulging IRA assuring the opportunity to travel without fear of bankruptcy. Quite the contrary. For us to embark on such a Journey required some rather involved planning. It also called for my Spiritual side to embrace a certain measure of faith unfortunately balanced by the human side expressed by the occasional knocking of my knees.

After losing Matt to cancer and engaging in much prayer (and a tremendous amount of conversation), Shaunda and I came to believe that God would have us invest at least two years telling this incredible story of hope and God's unbelievable grace. And with that, the preparations began.

A return to Dave Ramsey's "rice and beans, beans and rice" philosophy combined with the sale of the family home and liquidation of the majority of our possessions ensued. Subtract two cars and add a fifth wheel and truck, then live in the fifth wheel for a couple years to ensure that an aggressive savings program could be included in the dream. Just before our target date of March 6, 2016 we had placed enough money back to cover insurances as well as basic living incidentals. This placed the dream within reach. We could now drive a hundred miles to the megachurch with deep pockets and tell Matt's story. We could also drive a thousand miles to share with the assembly of forty and encourage their Pastor, when they could not spare one dime. And there is the dream: anytime, anywhere.

The other meaning of JOURNEY OF A LIFETIME? The premise that the life we live is in itself a Journey. It is often mirrored by a physical Journey. Some days are filled with bright sunshine and the promise of an early spring. Others are replete with angry storms, lightning, wind and rain. At times we become lost in the sunny day and are somehow shocked when the clouds form unexpectedly, in what seems like a moment. Other times we feel trapped by flooded roads or plagued by endless detours. If these seem so similar, what could we learn from the outside "Journey" that would help us better understand the inside "Greater Journey". The book you are reading is about both Journeys. First, is our one chance at an unbelievable "Journey of a Lifetime", and the second being the entirety of our individual Journey that *is* our life.

Want to see how all that works? Read on!

CHAPTER 29
THE SOUND IN THE SILENCE

As we often love to do when we are at the front end of a lot of miles, we like to space out the long travel days with an extra day in between. This approach delivers a much needed break and a chance to rest up. These "off days" present an opportunity to explore roadside attractions and oddities usually missed when "flying by" at interstate highway speeds. Pulling a 40' fifth wheel can be a bit stressful for us, so we like to keep our daily drives in the 250-300 mile range. When you factor in the mileage our diesel truck provides while pulling, this also allows us to unhook and then fuel up, eliminating the added stress of negotiating truck stops. Except, that is, when you are driving in a west direction into a stiff west wind. That setup ensures a fuel stop considering this day's mileage averaged only single digits.

Near Monahans Texas, just east of our intended destination for the night, we pulled into a beautiful new rest area to take care of necessities and stretch our legs. Inside the rest area was the outline of a world war two bomber that, by the way, seemed quite a bit out of place. With the investment of only a few minutes I was introduced by way of a historical plaque to the Rattlesnake Bomber Base. Ever heard of it?

Me neither. The brief interstate pit stop did however engender enough of an interest in this new discovery that it determined the destination for our foray on the upcoming day of rest.

Our stopover was confirmed for Pecos Texas. Pecos is a small oil town near the confluence of I-10 and I-20. Our extra day called for a drive through real Texas oil country. When you consider our timing included a possible oil boom on the horizon, to say the least, everything was full...full to overflowing. On this drive we passed a convoy of, in the vocabulary of a non-oil person, oil stuff. By stuff I mean trucks of all description, wide loads carrying huge tanks and entire office buildings. By convoy, I mean more than a mile of bumper-to-bumper traffic lumbering behind the office buildings on wide load flatbeds. In addition, the next 20 miles was a continuous flow of similar vehicles interspersed with dozens of all white, fleet style pickups.

We soon arrived at the spot marking the location of yesterday's discovery, though it is now long crumbled into the desert sand. The main gate to the bomber complex has been salvaged and restored.

The other remainders of this historically invaluable location rise up from the desert floor like the skeleton of a long forgotten hero.

It was this very location, entirely sequestered from the remainder of the America, where literally thousands of America's best young men trained to fly the bombers of World War 2. Consequently, they found themselves entirely sequestered from their friends, wives and parents as well. They learned to deliver their payloads in giant multi-engine bombers not even dreamed of a few years earlier. They would then soar over this seemingly endless stretch of nearly totally desolate land. Soon they will put their newly acquired skills to work over the cities and factories of Nazi Germany helping to crush perhaps one of the most godless regimes in history. Yes, thousands of young boys trained here…and thousands of young American men crossed the Atlantic to do their part to crush tyranny and enslavement. Others would fly over the Pacific to do battle with the unspeakable brutality of the Rising Sun. Thousands of these men would never again return to knock on their family's front door. Instead a smartly clad officer accompanied by a Chaplain would knock in their stead. And then a gold star would appear in their picture window for all to see.

To stand in the brisk desert wind as I did today, is to hear the drone of the tires on Interstate 20 passing by. In front of me the whir of small westbound cars and the growl of large westbound trucks scream out "busy, busy, busy". To my rear the heretofore-unnoticed freight train cars rumble mindlessly eastbound to complete a schedule determined days or even months earlier. And then they all pass at once, and in the sudden quiet all that can be heard is once again the wind.

Yet, if one truly listens, there are other sounds that can be plainly heard. In a time long before an interstate system was ever conceived and trains ran on the power of steam, young men fired up massive engines; first on B-17s, later on B-29s. This place was lovingly named the "Rattlesnake Bomber Base" after the literally thousands of rattlesnakes dislodged when the dirt work was begun on the twin one and one half mile concrete runways. The base also boasted five large hangers, shops, warehouses, and living quarters. It would seem that at the pinnacle of World War 2, this base would house more than 6,000 officers and enlisted men either permanently assigned or temporarily attached. In addition, there were hundreds of civilians that came from all over the United States to work at the base.

After the war, the base was renamed Pyote Air Force Base and became an aircraft storage depot. It served as a storage facility for as many as 2,000 aircraft. Her most famous "resident"? The B-29 Superfortress named "Enola Gay" after her pilot's mother. Later, after serving during the cold war as a radar  installation in the early warning network, the base was finally ordered closed by the US Air Force in 1963.

As I stood by the road today it was strangely quiet except for the drone of the passing vehicles. Yet, if you choose to, you can still hear the distinct roar of the bombers that helped win the war. You might also hear the voices of the young men who flew them. The young men that heard the call to a greater journey and chose to make whatever sacrifices were called for.

THE GREATER JOURNEY...

So what about you? Can you hear the sounds in the silence or are your spiritual senses dulled by busy, busy, busy? Do you find yourself in the mindless pursuit of the "what" when you have long forgotten the "why"? We have a war to fight as well, ours in the realm of the unseen.

Have we forgotten that our calling is to submit to the Almighty and do our part to help to crush the most godless regime in all of eternity? Yes, thousands have done their part to crush the tyranny and enslavement that Satan desires to bring upon all mankind. They have given their last full measure of devotion to Jesus Christ, the only worthy One. And now they have awoken in His presence to join and sing: "glory and honor and praise to the Lamb for all eternity. For only He is worthy".

Again, what about you? When you close your eyes for the final time and your race is run, how will you be remembered? Will you be thought of merely as a busy westbound car in pursuit of a few thousand dollars more? Or will you be recalled as more of a mindless eastbound train car following thoughtlessly along paths firmly set years in advance, powered not by your own choice but merely following the power provided by someone else's engine.

THE GREATER JOURNEY continued...

Will you be remembered for going through the motions so you can enjoy one more drink, one more party, one more salacious liaison or simply one more session in front of your favorite video game?

On the other hand, will your friends and family be able to one day stand and hear the sound in the silence? Will they still hear your song of praise that you sang with your life?

This is the Greater Journey.

I know from where I stand today if I truly listen, I can still hear Chris Tomlin's familiar strain...

How great is our God, sing with me
How great is our God, all will see
How great, How great is our God

CHAPTER 30
The Second Rattle

I love to make people laugh. Only problem is, I'm not very good at it. Every once in a while, I will say something I truly believe is funny. When Shaunda doesn't laugh the conversation that follows goes something like this:

"Don't you think I'm funny?" I ask.

To which Shaunda will inevitably respond: *"you* think you are".

There is one other "slice of wisdom" that she likes to share. Shaunda assures me that if I have to explain something I think is funny, that it wasn't really funny to begin with. I tend to believe that you'll agree with her as you read on.

As you may recall, one of the early chapters I wrote was entitled THE FIRST RATTLE OUT OF THE BOX. I shared how our first experience on this JOURNEY OF A LIFETIME was drastically and gloriously altered right at the beginning when Keegan came to be a part of our family. The beauty in the changes we did not expect became obvious as we discovered how wonderful our moments were with Ben, Jodi and

Makenna while we awaited Keegan's arrival, and even more so afterwards. We soon realized how many amazing moments we would have missed had God not made those opportunities available, or if we had not chosen to embrace them. Now the "humor" part:

"Rattle"... Keegan... New babies like rattles... Get it? See the play on words? FIRST RATTLE... Never mind. Shaunda was right. Undeterred by reality however, I'll give it another go with the SECOND RATTLE.

I am writing this in the truck on the way back to the Southwest; yes *back*. When you travel as much as we do, the interior of a truck can at times become a "rolling office" of sorts. It serves as a very friendly workplace with an ever-changing view out the "office" windows. Each time I look up from the computer screen the world around me is entirely different. Other than that, it's not that much different except for the fact that I have an office chair that is both heated and cooled. Another welcome, yet unexpected benefit; it helps make the miles pass quickly.

Four days ago Shaunda and I were just getting settled in at our RV park in southern New Mexico. This would serve as our base of operations for a few weeks. During this time frame I was focusing on completing Book #2, STORIES FROM THE ROAD... LESSONS FROM LIFE AND DEATH. (This work, ON THE VIRGE, THE JOURNEY OF A LIFETIME is planned for Book #3). The mornings had been quite productive, the weather pleasant and I was on track. Finishing up a four hour early morning writing session and needing a break, we headed for lunch and an afternoon at the border.

Only thirty miles due south is the historic town of Columbus, New Mexico. It's a bit of a shame, but few folks even know its historical significance. Sadder still is the reality that many unfortunately also might identify "Khe Sanh" as a local oriental restaurant or "Frozen Chosin" as one's first choice of an iced beverage at their favorite coffee house. That however, is a subject for another day.

Barely south of Columbus, New Mexico is the International border with Mexico complete with a 24 hour border crossing. There is a parking lot provided where you can leave you car and enter Mexico via a pedestrian walkway. On the Mexican side is the small town of Los Palomas. On the advice of some fellow campers, we crossed the bridge and tried out a local eatery. It was of the quaint open-air variety. The food  was authentic, the weather delightful and the enchiladas were amazing. Our server was superior. After a reasonably priced lunch he came around with complimentary dessert and complimentary margaritas. We gladly received the former and graciously declined the latter.

The next morning offered similar beginnings, a few hours of early morning writing accompanied by a steaming pot of coffee. I then received a text message from my son, Joe. As you may recall from an earlier chapter, last summer provided us the opportunity to spend a few weeks with Joey and Tacha in Colorado. It was during the very beginnings of an exciting time for them. They had just found out they were expecting their first child. The trip was memorialized for me when I held up four fingers and the shutter snapped in my ear. The resulting snapshot was of Tacha, Shaunda and me; only three. Yet there  was a fourth human being in the frame, although as of yet unseen; hence the title of the picture, "Four". The arrival of "four" was scheduled for a few weeks from what was now.

All the extended families had the "baby thing" pretty well planned out with regard to schedules, arrivals and duration of grandparent visits. Our dates were a bit fluid, but due to a multiplicity of factors, Shaunda and I had already determined that we would likely not be there for the "event". I went ahead and planned this tour, made the appropriate commitments and we started out on YEAR 2. Joe Jr. went on with a long ago scheduled work trip to Los Angeles. After all, it wasn't time for the baby just yet. A text message that morning would change everything for everybody.

After receiving this text, I immediately called Joe Jr., Shaunda immediately called Tacha. Shaunda and I compared notes while in the midst of our makeshift four-way phone call. I continued talking with Joey trying to extract details. Shaunda figured things out much quicker that I (unfortunately for me, this is not an uncommon occurrence). As I talked on the phone while looking at the weather forecast for a few key cities between the Mexican Border and central Colorado, Shaunda was busy stuffing t-shirts and necessities into a folding travel bag we keep in the storage area under our bed. It's kind of like while I was trying to make a decision, she was loading the truck.

A quick mileage check revealed that based on our current location, we were actually closer to our Colorado destination than had we been at home; more than five hours closer. Another winter snowstorm had battered the east leaving in its wake a myriad of cancelled and delayed flights, including Texas where Tacha's mom lives. Joe Jr. would be coming from southern California. There were no available flights from LAX to the tiny airport in the tiny town near his home. He would have to fly to Denver and then drive more than four hours. In Colorado. In the winter. Over Monarch Pass.

Just that quickly, we were the closest family. And just that quickly I heard the shutter click. You know what I mean, right? The sound that your smart phone makes virtually via a .wav file, or your DSLR makes when you press the red button. It's the sound of the camera shutter opening and closing. It results in a snapshot. A moment forever frozen in time. In my heart I knew right then that *this* moment in time was a gift from God, a "God moment" if you will. It would not be the last one to envelop my spirit over the next few days.

Soon we were on a nonstop drive to Colorado. Soon the 70+ degree temperatures of that streetside Mexican café would be traded for a Colorado morning low of 1 degree. The emotional electricity in the cab of our truck was palpable. No worries. Even had the electricity started a fire, our tears would have quickly put it out. The Colorado DOT website showed only green along our planned route indicating dry roadways. The extended weather forecast indicated a few days respite between the record central Colorado snowstorms that had begun just before Christmas and continued through the the following weeks.

Stopping only for fuel, restrooms and a single deli sandwich, which we split, on we drove. At the same time in Colorado, Joe Jr. and Tacha's back up plan was working flawlessly. Pre-prepared friends would arrive and function as surrogate family. While we were all on our way, a quick trip to the doctor for Tacha and an even quicker trip to the hospital only confirmed Shaunda's initial suspicions. This child would have none of our schedules or plans. Somewhere on a lonely Colorado Highway travelling at a few miles above the legal speed limit, the heavens opened for us as a seconds old snapshot appeared in my inbox. Click. I could almost hear the snap of the heavenly shutter.

It was dark when we pulled onto the icy parking lot at the small Colorado hospital. I was talking to Joe Jr. on the phone when he miraculously pulled in right behind me. Seems that when he calculated his arrival time, he hadn't factored in the time difference from the west coast. We arrived no more than two minutes apart.

 I followed him into the hospital. I followed him because I could not physically catch him. He was running. In less than two minutes I would enter a small birthing room only to be greeted by a smiling Mother. In the corner was my son, already holding a tiny bundle of life in his shaking arms. He was weeping, so I joined him.

In that moment I realized that perhaps one of the few things better in life than holding your new Grandchild in your arms, is watching the baby you held in your arms hold his baby in his. As I slipped down beside him on the small couch to get a better look, I realized that there was also an eternal connection. For although unseen in the room, there was another Father present, this one of the heavenly variety. My heavenly Father had held me in his arms long before I ever held my earthly son. I imagined a viewing stand in heaven as well, when all of the dots came together in an eternal instant. When they connected, they framed a picture that the greatest of this world's photographers could only dream of. And then the shutter clicked. Another God moment. An unspeakable blessing forever frozen in time. This time however, I noticed that Shaunda was holding my camera. This shutter click was real.

The next couple of days would yield many more "heavenly snapshots". Moments captured while sitting in a busy "locals" restaurant waiting on breakfast and talking to your firstborn son. Then you all of a sudden realizing

that your conversation was way more like one you would have with your best friend than one you would have with your child. Click.

Or like the snapshot taken when I held Nora Grace in my arms, or when the front door burst open and I watched this newly defined family come home for the very first time.

Or how about the pride this husband felt as he watched the love of his life busy herself with grocery shopping and all the preparations that our new mother never had the chance to complete; all because this child just wouldn't wait on her earthly appointed time of arrival. For a couple short days shutters were clicking all around me with a fervor that would eclipse a presidential news conference.

Soon airline schedules would cooperate and Tacha's mom would arrive. Soon it would be time to say "so long", climb back in the truck where I am writing these words, and once again head southwest. Thanks Nora for coming early. Or then again, perhaps you were right on time. You certainly demonstrated perfect timing to give "Poppi and Ma" a lifetime's worth of "God Moments". Moments forever frozen in time.

Thank you God for the "SECOND RATTLE OUT OF THE BOX".

And to think there was a time just a few years ago when I thought I might never smile again.

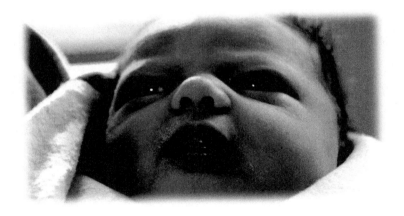

THE GREATER JOURNEY...

Does God care about the small things in our lives, or only the big ones? Read these verses and see what you think...

> *Matthew 10:29-31*
> *1 Peter 5:7*
> *Jeremiah 1:5*

What are some of your "God moments"?

CHAPTER 31
Tired Of Being Tired?

Let's just say that since we started this tour it's been the busiest six weeks of the Journey, most of it "non-bloggable". Hey, Did I just make up a word? Didn't think so.

Here's an overview: ONE Greater Journey Live Worship Event, ONE Stories From The Road Live Worship Event, ONE additional worship service, ONE book to the final edit process, THREE cuts for a new CD, ONE new grandchild, TWO funerals (Shaunda's family) and over FOUR THOUSAND miles on the odometer accomplishing all the above.

I'm tired. There is no complaint in there at all. I am thrilled to find myself still in the ministry and playing a part in people's lives. Honestly, it's not within my ability to try and explain how this makes me feel. I can't find the words. An earlier chapter may help you understand, provided you remember it. It's just that I'm tired.

We made it back to New Mexico from Colorado and "The Virge" a few days ago, already past our checkout date at the RV Park. Graciously our "home" was still there and had not been removed to the local police impound. We extended our stay for a couple days to get rested up a bit and then headed out on the eight-hour run to Big Bend. Ever been tired but not tired? Ever been tired and tired? Ever been tired of being tired?

I'm also thrilled to find myself enjoying a bit of R&R while working on some smaller projects. Speaking of that, we were off to Big Bend National Park today to see if we might get lost in the wilderness. I'll just bet I can make that happen. Sometimes I get lost just driving to the store and back.

I thought I had been to National Parks before (fifteen at last count on this JOURNEY OF A LIFETIME alone), but five minutes into Big Bend National Park made me question that a bit. So many of the parks we've been to hold breathtaking beauty along with bumper-to-bumper traffic. Big Bend holds all of the former with none of the latter. This is one of the least visited National Parks in the nation and also one of the largest. The sum of that equation is wide-open spaces. I suppose yearly visitation is low here because this place is not on the way to anywhere nor around the corner from anything. Again, both factors play to exactly what I needed in my spirit right now as we begin to consider whether there will be a YEAR 3 at all. Hard to believe it's already really time to think about this.

I imagine that all those factors played into our first real decision of the day. With end of February morning temperatures already approaching 80 degrees and with the bright sunshine streaming down unabated by the smallest of clouds, we were presented with a choice. Grab the backpack that contained hastily prepared sandwiches, water and some fruit and head down a trail, or walk up a small incline and grab a seat on the beautiful patio at the lodge restaurant. Keep in mind I am still a bit tired.

When it came time for the decision on today's lunch, for me it was a no brainer. I was not tired, but I was still tired. Got the double speak figured out yet? There is a physical tired and there is an emotional tired. One tends to influence the other. After long periods of either, or both, we can become tired of being tired. One might describe that state of mind as weariness.

Decision made. In one motion I grabbed the ever-ready hiking backpack and we headed down the trail. I glanced at the sign that gave explicit instructions on how to ward off a bear attack and its sister sign that gave similar advice in how to deal with mountain lions. Within a few minutes the loudest sounds I could hear were the clump of my boots hitting the rocks in a steady rhythm perfectly mixed with the call of a dozen wrens. Talk about music. Now that, my friends, proved to be a musical creation that could rival the greatest of symphonies.

On we walked up a mountain trail and around corners surrounded by trees that filtered the bright sunshine, subdividing it into a hundred different beams. Then in the middle of our path stood a gigantic fourteen-foot tall grizzly bear. He was standing straight up on his hind legs with razor like claws extending at least twelve inches from his hands. He growled loudly: "Do you have a banana or an orange?"

OK, none of the last half of that paragraph really happened; I just wanted to make sure you were still listening. If you're not too angry with me, please read on.

No bear, but we did enjoy a great lunch at the apex of the trail. From that point I could clearly see where two portions of the Chios Mountains came together yielding an enormous "V". This provided a natural frame for an unbelievable view off into the vastness the mountains had been hiding. Looking out dozens of miles into that immense wilderness a strange thought occurred to me. I was getting a little tired from the climb, yet I was far less tired in the other way than I had been for days. Let me put it this way. I became "tired" during the seemingly endless monotonous drive through West Texas. That tired was being wiped away by the beauty of the expanse that lay out before me.

I'm going to tread out on some potentially volatile ground here, so read carefully. I don't want to kindle the ire of any scholar or geologist, nor do I desire to engender a discussion on creation verses evolution. However, did you ever notice that at times science pits itself against God? Like last night when I lay on my back under the Texas dark skies and within a few minutes I saw more stars than I have ever seen in one night in my entire life. Perhaps more stars than I have ever seen in every other night of my life combined. While one secular scientist may see random chance, I see intelligent design. Likewise, in few places is this difference of interpretation more evident than in our National Parks.

I don't offer an intended argumentative point here, rather a thought for your consideration. I see one thing, and then I see the Creator of that thing because I believe in a Creator. The godless look at the same thing and see 60 million years, often because they don't believe in a Creator in the first place. Those 60 million years (or 150 million, or 2 billion) allow plenty of time for random chance to result in what they see. This eliminates the need of any Creator at all. If we can eliminate God altogether, then we can eliminate any standard of righteousness from our lives. This in turn eliminates any requirement to behave in a way other than what our darkened hearts dictate. This is why the world system fights so hard for evolution, abortion and humanism. Any missing piece from their puzzle, and the rest of it falls apart. This requires they come face to face with God. And this is what they call "freedom"?

While they see "60 million years of evolutionary and geologic force at work", I see the mighty hand of God scooping out the indescribably beautiful valley that lay before me. While they see ancient cosmic explosions resulting in the stars twirling randomly overhead, I envision the fingertips of God flinging the heavenly bodies into the exact places He desired them to be. I can't help but wonder how different our world's condition might be if the plaques in the Parks read differently. Instead of "60 million years ago on this spot...", what if the opening lines were "If you walked into this magnificent place doubting the existence of God, take a moment and look through out between these mountains...".

As I continued following the predetermined path, I realized that a position with head raised, constantly scanning the horizon was not the best choice. It was then that I tripped on the rocks and ran squarely into tree limbs. I was also reminded that a gaze fixed squarely on the path yielded a more stable walk, but simultaneously robbed me of the ability to view the splendor all around me.

The answer to this dilemma? This is one of the keys to successfully living the Christian life. It is also the most often overlooked. Balance and rest. Assure yourself of the path ahead only for the next steps. Only then raise your head and breathe deeply of the Journey. Then quickly drop your head again to make certain of the path. Then when you get "tired", stop and rest. Have a bite of lunch. Here, give no thought to the path, only the Journey.

Just as certain as those two days of physical recovery in New Mexico solved my first "tired", drinking deeply of the Journey solved my second. While some may look through that "window" and see geologic history and explainable formations, I see something unspeakably simpler, and yet unfathomably more complex. I see God.

Around one of the final corners I noticed that Shaunda, although smiling, was appearing a bit winded. "You okay?" I asked.

"Oh yeah" came the response. "I'm just tired".

Before engaging my "sense of humor brake", I said: "But it's a good tired, right?"

Her quick glance said it all without ever speaking a word. It's the same expression I saw on her face only a few weeks earlier when Nathaniel, a Pastor in

Southern Arizona, said: "Yeah, but it's a dry heat". I witnessed it in Colorado a couple weeks ago when it was all of 1 degree and Joe Jr. said: "Yeah, but it's a different kind of cold". At that moment it was clear that what Shaunda was really saying, "there is no good tired (or dry heat or different cold)". Although I am on truly dangerous ground now, I would venture that at a much deeper level there is really is a "good tired".

For me it's the tired I feel when we have just completed a successful LIVE WORSHIP EVENT where hearts have been touched. With the equipment finally loaded, the Virge hooked up and often after we have shared a meal and a goodbye hug with new friends, we drive off into the night. I am tired, but it's a good tired.

Perhaps its when the long time retiree who refuses to be retired and instead works long hours in volunteer construction to provide a place for Christians to worship or kids to go to camp. Only later he falls into his recliner tired, but a good tired.

Maybe it's the Pastor who invests himself emotionally, spiritually and physically into a group of people week after week. Then he returns home to invest emotionally in his family. He gives and gives until he is tired, but a good tired.

It could be the mom who through no fault of her own has endured a devastating divorce. In place of trips to the salon for a pedicure she now rises up even earlier in the mornings to straighten up the house and lay out food for supper. Then she drops the children off at school and only then shows up for a full day's work.

After work takes its toll she returns home, helps with homework, pays the bills and does everything possible to make a stable home for her hurting children. Then she falls into bed, tired and alone. But it's a good tired.

Perhaps it's the mom who turned her back on a job making more money than I will ever make simply (but not really "simply") to stay at home and raise children. A lady who makes a choice to radically lessen the scope of her world and exchange it for a life of what is ostensibly more obscure. When she finally has a moment to herself, she will find herself tired, but a good tired.

Bad tired is when that single parent turns for relief to alcohol instead of Christ. It's when that "stay at home mom" feels that she is having little effect and contemplates giving up. When the Pastor sheds quiet private tears feeling unappreciated and taken for granted while feeling like a captive in a church that will never be as large as the one down the street. It's when the retiree feels like he is just spinning his wheels and accomplishing little of real value. He figures he might just as well hang up his hammer and accept the reality that his years have outlasted their ability to contribute. It's when this Journeyer says he may be nearing the end of a great Journey and its time to move on to somewhere new.

But Godly reality is found in balance and rest. It's not time to *give* up, its time to *look* up. Its time to open our eyes on the vastness and power of a God that can merely, by the power of His word, speak a world like ours into existence.

Today if you are tired, or if you are "tired", or perhaps you are even tired of being tired, here's a word of great hope. I heard a voice yesterday and it still calls out to me today… and to you as well. "Come to me, all you who are weary and burdened, and I will give you rest". Matthew 11:28

Add to this hike, two (yes 2) more hikes along with more quick stops along the scenic highway than I can count. Top it off with an unbelievable sunset as we approached one of the last grades before our RV park and you have one pretty amazing day. So if I personally am really tired (physically), but not tired (emotionally), why is it that I just can't seem to close my eyes? Maybe I just don't want to miss one moment of this Journey of a Lifetime.

THE GREATER JOURNEY...

Read Matthew 11:28-30.

In verse 28 Matthew invites the weary and burdened to find rest. In verse 29, he gives us even a little deeper insight by adding one thought. Walking with Christ will provide rest FOR YOUR SOULS.

How would you describe being weary in your soul?

Here's an idea. If you have ever struggled with this kind of tired, why not commit these verses to memory. You may be surprised at how God can use His word when it is ingrained in your memory.

Matthew 11:28-30
28 "Come to me, all you who are weary and burdened, and I will give you rest.29 Take my yoke upon you and learn from me, for I am gentle and humble in heart, and you will find rest for your souls. 30 For my yoke is easy and my burden is light."

CHAPTER 32
Will There Be A YEAR 3?

Now well into YEAR 2, there is one burning question on the hearts and minds of everyone today. OK, not everyone's mind, but it sure is on mine. With every tick of the clock the answer to this question is beginning to take on new importance, for me that is. There is nothing magical per se about this JOURNEY OF A LIFETIME being a two-year adventure, it is way more about the combination of believing that God has only led us for these first steps, along with simple mathematics.

That being said, I'm trying to hedge my bets just in case. Every church we go to I drop off a resume. It says something like: "very, very, very, very, very experienced Worship Leader. Pretty fair piano player, but looks nasty in skinny jeans". Never hurts to be prepared.

Like most everyone else's life, our lives tend to be "boundaried by budget". Several years ago now when we sold our home and liquidated the majority of our belongings, life became a great deal simpler. We purchased our truck and fifth wheel and set about preparing for the future. We would need adequate funding for camping, fuel and food, as well as for the basic necessities; those "necessities" being primarily our insurances (truck, rv, and medical). We were able to save two years worth of projected expenses ourselves by funding two bank accounts, one for each of these categories (expenses and insurances). In this way, we could function within our mission statement of "anytime, anywhere" to tell Matt's story without asking for anything; except the opportunity to share that is.

Funding this ministry at its basic level requires only these two categories be considered. To continue into the future however (YEAR 4 and on), would also call for preparations to replace our road equipment (fifth wheel and/or truck). While we prepared before we ever left for these things for the two years, we are living in the margin, as this equipment will not last indefinitely. Unfortunately, I no longer have a regular income to purchase another truck and trailer.

All these factors considered together leave the determination of a year three or beyond based on an affirmative answer to each of three questions. Ready? Here we go.

FIRST... Is there funding?
To continue, we would need to do our best to ensure we have enough money. This could come from one or more of several different revenue streams. Here are some possibilities:

> • The offerings from the churches where we tell Matt's story is one such stream.

• We have not asked for anyone to support this ministry, even after the establishment of our 501(c)(3); yet some have, and we are very grateful. Tax-exempt gifts from concerned individuals and/or corporations is another possible "stream".

• A few churches have considered supporting us monthly from their Missions budgets. This is another possible source.

• People who would respond in person at our LIVE WORSHIP EVENTS with an offering when each book or CD project released is yet another.

• Book and music sales is another great income source, but as you recall, we have intentionally chosen not to market books or music in the traditional manner. However, offerings recieved when each book or CD project released is an equally great opportunity for us.

• Expanding the scope of this ministry to include GATEKEEPERS (church safety) and/or Media and Music Creation and Church Music Consulting are other possibilities as well.

The bottom line is simple. We are not wealthy people and common sense dictates that we cannot go without income indefinitely. And though some might consider this next statement arrogant at best or ignorant at worst, we are simply not going to ask for money. I just don't want to be "that guy". You know, the guy on the TV constantly begging for your money.

God may use any or all of these, or something entirely different. I figure He already knows. He can handle this.

SECOND... *Do we have anywhere to go?*
The entire budget of the world is pretty much useless if we don't have anywhere to tell the story. We have had a good first year with repeat invitations at 100%. If YEAR 2 shows a similar success, we should be well on our way to establishing the base of supporting churches that would justify a YEAR 3. If at anytime God closes the spigot, that would be a pretty good indicator that our time is up.

THIRD...*Do we want to do this any longer?*
Or, if you prefer a more "spiritual approach", do we believe God still wants us to continue.

Well, there you have it. Those are the three criteria we are considering from which to arrive at a decision.

If we decide that it's a "two and through" scenario, that will give us a few months before the funding runs out for me to seek gainful employment. Keep me in mind in case that's the route we end up going. After all, by that time I'll be a year older and there will be one more "very" in front of that "experienced".

CHAPTER 33
Too Much

Well, here's a chapter I knew I would have to write sometime, I just wasn't in any hurry. As in every Journey, even this one, there are times when circumstances dictate outcomes that are less than we wish they would be. This Journey, like every Journey, is not all happiness. This first tour of YEAR 2, to this point, could be construed as something like that.

This JOURNEY OF A LIFETIME, when most fulfilling, calls for a specific recipe. The main ingredient is the story. Without the story, there would be no Journey. But as in any good meal, being served only the main ingredient assures a collective "blah" from any partaker. We need to add some spice, perhaps some additional ingredients. Here's what we've discovered our "recipe" to be: combine two parts Journey, with one part destination, then spice with various adventures. Thoroughly mixed, we can dish out a scrumptious portion of the JOURNEY OF A LIFETIME.

Beginning with the planning stages for this first tour of YEAR 2, for whatever reason, difficulty has been our travel companion. While I realize that the Story part (the main ingredient if you will), is not an every weekend occurrence, it suffices to say that the opportunities have been a bit sparse so far for this second tour. While the rest of the year is shaping up a bit better, the slow start is a bit disconcerting, *too* disconcerting.

Truthfully, I have had plenty to keep me busy. Preparing STORIES FROM THE ROAD for printing, recording and mixing the accompanying music project and working on several small projects have filled the days. The weather has been awesome. To describe the hikes and the unbelievable scenery here in the Big Bend region of Texas requires a thesaurus larger than I have access to. It's just that the main ingredient is missing. It's really got me down, *too* down.

The approach I took for booking this tour was not much different than what I employed in the first two. We were invited to a few places and I was able to secure some additional opportunities around them. I was also able to sit back and watch God fill in a few dates as well. It's just that for the first time several of those opportunities have fallen through, and all of them on this tour. I also watched God remain eerily silent. To be completely transparent, we're not talking about the cancellation of actual confirmed dates here, we're talking about the "when you're coming this way let me know" kind, and the "I think that will work, let me get back with you" kind. It's just that the dates didn't work out, while others "forgot" to call back. And just like that, the main ingredient was MIA. I really became a bit irritated, *too* irritated.

It's not a money thing. Remember, we're in YEAR 2 of a Journey God allowed us to fund entirely in advance, so that's not the issue. It's more of a "rejection" issue.

My character flaws are such that I can't seem to help but take it personally. It simply makes me feel bad, *too* bad.

Truth is: we're already ahead of where we were last year at this time. We are in a beautiful part of the country. We have several opportunities already scheduled for the rest of the year. Why, I even detailed my truck yesterday. That always makes me feel better.

Keep in mind that mixed in with this mess is the reality that my age presents. Remember the "skinny jean" thing? Truth is, that is just a humorous way for me to acknowledge the fact that I am, shall we say, not as able to compete in the workforce at the level I once was. Yet I am neither old enough nor wealthy enough to retire. There is a several year gap between A & B.

I just don't understand why it is that all this is affecting me in such a dramatic way. While mulling over these details and doing my best to understand the "why" of my distressing mood, one overriding fact became glaringly obvious. It's not odd that these things would bother me, it's just that I am *too* bothered. I am *too* disconcerted. I am *too* down. I am *too* angry. I feel *too* bad. Why all the "*toos*"? It's all just too much.

You've likely already figured out that there is a glaringly absent element in my thought process. Faith seems to be missing entirely, replaced instead by a grim vision of the future. I learned many years ago that the only way to fight "feelings" is with "facts" (You can read about all that in STORIES FROM THE ROAD). So what are the "facts" that must be considered in understanding my "feelings"? Had I ever felt like this before?

The first real loss I remember was my paternal grandmother. My maternal grandmother was already in a long-term care facility at my earliest recollection, and she soon passed away. Both my grandfathers were gone before I was born. In 1973, when I was sixteen, my Grandma Knight passed away. I'm sure I cried that day, but what I remember most is that my dad cried. I had never seen that before. I knew one thing for sure, I couldn't quite understand.

My next major loss was my mom in 1988. My dad followed in 1995. I remember vividly when my mom passed away from cancer. As I sat by her bed on that last, seemingly endless night, I finally understood why my dad had cried so many years earlier. Laugh if you wish, or roll your eyes if that helps you with this next statement, but I realized that I had just lost the only person who really knew what I was like when I was in Junior High. Sounds silly I know, but for whatever reason, that stuck out to me. Perhaps its because during those years of my life I was indeed was type of person that "only a mother could love".

My mom passed in September. A few days later I returned to Springfield Missouri, where I had just begun a new ministry, and I threw myself into my work. I had just started on staff of a large, well known Church. This task would require all there was of me, and I wanted to give it, unreservedly. (By the way, for you TEARS IN A BOTTLE folks, does that "busyness" sound at all vaguely familiar? Seems like I really didn't learn that lesson the first time around.) The weeks passed quickly however, and I was soon adapting to this new world, a world without my mother.

I remember to this day one particular Monday in early November of that year. The sun shone brightly that morning, but my internal sun was unreasonably dim. I got dressed for work and pulled out of the driveway unable to comprehend the reason for the darkness; the darkness that was now rapidly progressing in my soul. Arriving at work, I entered my office, sat down behind the giant wooden desk (Earl Smith's desk) and proceeded to do... nothing. I had now entered into a realm of darkness that had overtaken my spirit.

A casual glance at the calendar brought about unexpected, yet immediate clarity. It was Monday morning, November 7, 1988. This was my mother's birthday. The internal well opened up and within moments the tears had washed the darkness from my soul.

Last week while sitting in a folding lawn chair in the hot West Texas sun, I was looking all around me at the beautiful, yet desolate mountain landscape when it first dawned on me. It was reasonable that the circumstances I was thinking about concerned me. It was the "too" in all those emotions and the borderline desperation that concerned me most. My emotion was inappropriate for my reality. It was simply too much.

As quickly as your bathroom light responds to the flip of a switch, I realized that just like so many years earlier, this was all brought about not at all by the circumstances, but rather by the calendar. It is the first week of March. We were slowly approaching March 15th, the date of Matt's death.

To clarify, March fifteenth has over the years become a relatively easy day. To be completely honest, it was not really that bad of a day back in 2009. It was a Sunday morning and Matt passed away shortly after midnight. That Sunday would be the only one I missed leading worship in the entirety of that Journey. By 4am we were packed, pulling out of the "apartment" parking garage and heading back to Greenville. As horrible as this may sound to you, I was in many ways relieved. Relieved for sure to finally be going home. Relieved for sure that Matt was finally "home" as well. Relieved that this horrible nightmare was over. But most relieved, as you might well imagine, that Matt was no longer suffering. No longer struggling. No longer laboring to breathe. No longer seemingly suspended between earth and heaven.

I can't explain this, but March the 15th has held relief for me nearly every year since. That date calls to remembrance Matt's deliverance. In the same way, nearly every year, the two weeks before March 15th have held inordinately strong and dark emotions. Those weeks call to remembrance Matt's suffering.

This year, eight years down the road, is the first year since Matt passed away that we have faced these dates alone. For years, whether they ever knew it or not, we intentionally placed ourselves around friends and family. You may recall that last year, on YEAR 1 of this Journey, we spent this day with Makenna on her Spring break. That was no accident either. This year, in YEAR 2, I planned to be right here in Big

Bend. But for whatever reason the meticulously slow lumbering of the calendar combined with the recent unexpected fast pace of life brought about by births and deaths had caused the reason for this planned absence to completely slip my mind.

As a Law Enforcement Chaplain I have sat across living rooms and dining room tables with more families than I can recall, dealing with their intense loss. I have shared with them two lessons I learned from others, and have since learned for myself. First, You never get *over* a loss of this kind, but you can get *through* it. And second, although it never quits hurting, over time the pain lessens in intensity and does not last nearly as long. If that doesn't sound like hope to you, you haven't been buried deep enough in loss... yet. Those two statements form what I would come to know as "genuine hope with a strong dose of reality".

Somehow, just realizing there is an elephant in the room, and acknowledging that he is there, goes a long way to arriving at the ultimate reality. The reality that this elephant, while large, ugly and at times a bit smelly, is actually quite powerless. For the believer, death has *no* real sting and there is *no* victory in the grave.

True, death will come and snatch away those we love the most. True, we have no longer the joy of walking beside them, the chance to share in conversation or the opportunity to work out the intricacies of a musical arrangement. But they are not lost. If I lose my sunglasses (and I seem to do that quite often) they are only lost if I don't know where they are. Once Shaunda reminds me that she just saw them lying on the kitchen counter, they are no longer lost. I am only separated from them until I get back home. Separation though painful, is anything but final. It ends entirely and forever when we get "home".

Each time we face a deeper loss in our lives we discover a corresponding new depth of sadness. We also discover the reality that the Grace of God is sufficient for, well, anything. The memory of that pain can replay itself complete with the accompanying stab of fear that can literally take our breath away all over again. Yet, we also have the reality that we are never truly alone. He is a friend that is closer than a brother. He never leaves us. His strength is shown complete in our weakness. Even when it seems He is silent.

On that morning in Big Bend country, once again the wellspring of the grace of God rose up from my soul and washed away the encroaching darkness. I'd like to tell you more, but I think I just heard Shaunda call for me. She has the bicycles ready for us on the concrete patio of our campsite here at Big Bend. And that brings a smile to my face. A smile that had been missing for several days.

I guess that the reality of His unending grace is just "too much" for the fears that assault our souls.

THE GREATER JOURNEY...

I'm on dangerous ground here. I never claimed to be a professional counselor or to possess any significant training in that area. I am merely a fellow journeyer, one who has experienced a bit of life's pain and heartache.

I have no idea where you are on your Journey as you read this. I know not your specific pain be it financial, relational, personal or any other kind.

I cannot promise you that tomorrow will be better. I cannot offer any explanation for your struggle or any clever words to alleviate your suffering.

I can, however, share some living and powerful words in which you can unreservedly place your confidence, for they are not my words.

Hebrews 13:5   Proverbs 18:24   1 Peter 5:7
Revelation 21:4

CHAPTER 34
The Unthinkable
(By Shaunda)

Well into our Journey we had the opportunity to sing at a beautiful church in Eureka Springs Arkansas. In an earlier chapter Joe told you about his friend and fellow Pastor who is a licensed psychologist. He pastors this church and it was a real blessing to watch him and Joe reconnect after being separated for many years.

After the services the four of us had the chance to spend a lot of hours together. This Pastor's wife is a wonderful person and is a credit to Pastor's wives everywhere. We sat down in their home after church where I was introduced to the game of Rook, and introduced to potato chips, dips and more desserts that you can imagine. Talk about the perfect evening!

Joe warned me ahead of time to keep an eye on this man. With Joe's warning that he was a "real psychologist" he told me not to answer any questions that began with "how do you feel about...". The question he asked me didn't start like that, so I was blindsided.

Without any warning, he looked right at me and said: "I understand what Joe is trying to get across to people in your program" he began, "but what do you hope people will learn from Matt's story?"

"Wow" is all I could think. "Pass the brownies" was all I could think to say. It was a great question, and one that really forced me to think. Joe is the speaker, the singer and the writer. I handle the computer and talk to people privately. Not like, up in front.

Here was my answer that I shared that night. I think it surprised even Joe. I hope it helps and encourages you. If you are a Mother or Grandmother, I pray it challenges you as well. Here is one of the greatest lessons I learned. When Joe tells Matt's story, he always includes the part about Matt being a great athlete, and truly he was. To illustrate that point, Joe usually tells people that he "has the home run balls to prove it". We really do still have quite a few, but not as many as we used to. Each of the kids took some, but there are several left.

In the corner of a closet I have a small wooden box. I call it my "Matt box". In it are some pictures, a few of Matt's personal effects, some of his achievement certificates and awards... and a baseball. I was looking at these things one day when I was all by myself. When I held that baseball in my hand I realized a very important truth; when a person dies, they really don't take anything with them. Nothing. Certainly no trophies or awards. And certainly no baseballs.

The only thing that I ever had a part in giving Matt that he did take with him was Christ. The most important thing we can "give" our kids is to introduce them to the

Lord. If the unthinkable happens in your home as it did in mine, they won't take a single "Straight A" report card, academic or sport's trophy with them. It's not up to us to save our kids, but it assuredly is our responsibility to introduce them to Christ, to take them to church, and to make spiritual things a priority in their lives. A priority over sporting events or scholastic meets. You never know when they go to church camp, Sunday school or youth activity, if it will be the real life changer for them.

If you had asked me ten years ago, I would have told you this would never happen to any of our kids. They were all healthy. But how quickly that can change. If I were sitting across the couch from a young mom right now I would tell them to make Christ the single priority of their life. Words are important, actions are much more important. A child learns from seeing more than from hearing. If I wish for my child to make Christ a priority in their life, I must make Him the priority of mine.

Translated, that means instead of heading to the lake for some fishing, or going golfing, to the movie or just laying in bed on Sunday morning, get up and take your children to Church. Put down that secular novel and allow your children to catch you reading your Bible, every day. Turn off your favorite radio station and fill your home and your car with Christian music.

There is certainly nothing wrong with softball, baseball or most other activities. It can be good for your kids. Likewise there is nothing necessarily wrong with Pilates, yoga, workouts or a good pedicure. These can be good for you. There exists however, a grave danger when we allow busyness to fill our lives to the point where we worry more about running an efficient taxi service than providing a Godly home. It's OK to say no to any activity if that activity stands in the path that leads to your saying yes to God. Slow down, breathe, and hold your children close. We have no guarantee we will even be able to do that tomorrow.

Today I am grateful that I have an old battered baseball to hold in my hand and a box full of awards to look at. I am unbelievably more grateful that I have the assurance that Matt is with Christ. The next time you face one of these "priority decisions" for your children, or for you, put yourself in circumstances similar to mine. Then make the decision you will wish you had if this unthinkable tragedy should visit your home.

THE GREATER JOURNEY...

Read Matthew 6:33

This is a very familiar part of the Bible. Often when we read this, we focus on the last part, the "getting for us" part. The "all things will be added" part.

For today though, let's forget all that. Let's take a moment and look at only the first words. What practical choices can you make today to be certain that Christ is the singular priority of your life?

CHAPTER 35
How Funny

Shortly after March Madness was over, my personal March Madness that is, several fairly amazing things happened. Two days after Shaunda rolled the bicycles around the Fifth Wheel I booked four churches. Two days later, now past those ominous days leading up to March 15, I scheduled a couple more. Fast forward a few days, and a couple more requests came in and I found myself looking at only a handful of available Sunday mornings for the remainder of the year. Could this be the beginning of the "taking on a life of its own"?

Glancing at the Big Bend region of West Texas one final time through the large rear view mirrors on our truck, we continued on our Journey, now working back  towards our home base in East Texas. Avoiding the interstates, at least for a while, we chose instead to follow US Highway 90 winding it's way along the Rio Grande.

We were afforded an opportunity to tell a portion of Matt's story in San Antonio. On this Sunday I chose to use some of the elements of the GREATER JOURNEY Live Worship Event in conjunction with the Thanksgiving portion of our new STORIES FROM THE ROAD Live Worship Event. This hybrid presentation seemed to offer a real chance at "success". This was a medium sized Church with a very impressive attendance, especially for a Spring Break Sunday. In this unique Live Worship Event I began with a piano solo followed by an up-tempo worship tune that invites participation.

I met a day earlier with the Worship Leader to set sound, as is the norm. Although he was firmly anchored in the "skinny jean" generation, he was quite gracious and we hit it off pretty well. We moved their rich sounding grand piano a bit closer to the center of the platform, and then patched my small soundboard into their existing house system. Their sound system included two subwoofers that I'm not at all certain I could fit in the back of my truck. Tuning my system was easy as well. I switched on the spectrum analyzer and immediately noticed that nearly all the frequencies were visible and in their appropriate levels without adjusting the equalizer. Interpretation? It sounded really good.

My opening piano solo in this presentation amounts to two verses and a chorus of a familiar song. I present this in a solid, yet simplified, straightforward manner. No arpeggios, no fancy stuff. This portion uses a click trak that only I can hear in my in-ear monitors. The video shows nothing but a static picture on the screen; the logo image for STORIES FROM THE ROAD.

Interpretation here? This is the magic that allows the "orchestra" to enter on cue and the video to start mid stream in a song when no one really expects it.

On this morning, when my orchestra joined (the "midi" type of orchestra that is) the video began to stream corresponding images. The keyboard work became a bit more expressive and then this congregation shocked me. I think I could say that most leapt to their feet and began to applaud; from the beginning of the final chorus all the way through to the end of the piece.

Next was that up-tempo, participatory worship tune. I didn't ask anyone to sing. I didn't request that anyone clap along with the music. I didn't even request that they stand. I didn't have to ask for any of these. They did it all on their own. Better stated, I didn't have to even slightly encourage these folks to worship. It was more like all I needed to do was crank the engine and get out of the way.

How funny. They had no idea that this was the first Sunday that followed March fifteenth.   They had no idea how I had just struggled with my own personal "March Madness". They had no idea that they were exactly what my spirit needed. How funny.

I remember an old "quartet joke" from way back in my teen years when my music group travelled the quartet circuit a bit. I first heard it one Saturday evening at a high school auditorium somewhere in South Georgia. We opened for the Cathedral Quartet that night. We felt pretty good about ourselves as we set up our product table in the hallway and laid out our three records for sale. (Yes, "records". Ask someone you know who doesn't wear skinny jeans either and they will tell you about these audio relics.) We flanked them with pictures, t-shirts, cassettes and eight tracks (never mind). It all was displayed on a black, crushed velvet tablecloth with our logo embroidered across the front. We were all teenagers, but as far as the southern gospel quartet music world was concerned, we certainly had "arrived".

We completed our opening music set and then our lead singer made his "product speech". "Here's our three record albums" he would begin, "Ten dollars each, or all three for twenty". This was certain to bring in the cash. Then it was time for Glen, George and the Cathedrals to take the stage.

Anyone who has ever experienced an "Old fashioned Saturday Night Singin'" type of thing knows exactly what happened next. The volume on the sound system got cranked up 20db and the Cathedrals forevermore rocked the house. Youngsters, laugh all you want. Back in the day when we did this style of music, this *was* cutting edge. After the completion of thirty or so minutes by likely the greatest Southern Gospel quartet to ever file off a bus, they laid down their microphones and walked to the edge of the stage. With no sound reinforcement whatsoever, they added another fifteen minutes of overwhelmingly moving acapella hymns.

With a half dozen impressionable teenagers watching from backstage with lower jaws scraping the floor, Glen and George then delivered the coup d' grace. In their humorous style as only they could do, they presented their version of the "product speech". Filled with back and forth humor, they offered at least twenty different LPs. And then...wait for it... they presented their "blue light special". Any six records for $20.

SIX for $20, not THREE.

And then came the overused quartet joke.

"We only have a limited supply of these records," says the straight man.

"That's right", picks up the comedian. "And when those are gone we'll go back to the bus and get another limited supply".

Lesson in humility complete, I still remember hearing the uproarious laughter of the crowd echoing through the high school hallways as we slithered to our paltry product table and took our position behind the crushed velvet tablecloth. We were situated directly next to their giant tables of product surrounded by racks and racks of records. And the crowds came; and gathered around their table. I don't remember how much we sold in product that night, but I recall that it was not nearly enough to even begin to fill the bottomless pit that held the diesel fuel on our bus.

Now there you have it; one of the longest rabbit chases in literary history. This story did however, come back to me oddly enough, after the service at this wonderful Church in San Antonio while driving back to our Fifth Wheel.

I have not said a lot about our individual worship services since the beginning days of our Journey. It was then that, sad as it is, I was regularly overwhelmed by the presence of the Holy Spirit working through the power of Matt's story. Sad, that is, because as a career Worship Leader, this power tended to be the exception, not the rule. Let's just say that this type of extraordinary service has continued almost without exception. This Sunday in March was by no means an exception either. The power of Christ was nearly palpable as tears flowed freely from the hearts of worshippers. And a unique thing about this service? No one really knew Matt's story yet, nor did they realize how the calendar was playing into *our* lives.

After the opening songs, I spoke a bit about Matt and our two-year mission to tell his story. That was followed by another song and then a video. It was during that song that I first noticed a person get up and walk out of the worship center. "Oh great", I thought, "this awesome sound system is so potent that it is driving would be worshippers to the street". Or perhaps the Church leadership had served too much coffee and orange juice during Sunday School. Soon though, this person returned and sat down.

Then another worshipper got up and then soon returned. Then another and yet another. By that point I had given up trying to figure out what was going on and instead I focused on what I should have been thinking bout all along; Worship.

The service now complete, once again I had the opportunity to meet fellow Journeyers. In many churches, this portion of the time we get to spend is quite often the most moving for me. This day would be no exception. After shaking several hands and sharing in more than a few hugs, a really kind couple approached. They were my age, or perhaps a slight bit more. The distinguished lady began our conversation with some gracious words of encouragement. Soon however, I would learn that she and her husband were members of the same "club" as we were. This "club" as I came to call it, is not one that you would ever choose to be a part of. It, rather, chooses you.

I started calling it a "club" years ago, when the most diverse group of men you could imagine started having breakfast once a month at a  local eatery. They didn't attend my church. We didn't golf together or play poker; we actually had very little in common. There was a Judge and a mortician. There was a man who worked at a local business, and there was a preacher... me. Others joined from time to time. They were equally as diverse in background. Yet there was one powerful bonding element between us. We were all living the rest of our lives without our sons. My son's death was from cancer. Another's was murdered in a senseless act of violence. Still another's son gave his life in Iraq defending our freedom.

Occasionally we talked seriously. Mostly we laughed. Sometimes we cried. Typically we just listened to each other's stories and somehow it was enough just to know that we weren't alone on our Journeys. And there we sat, Monday after Monday, looking out the window watching the cars and trucks fly down the interstate. We were white men and black men. Young men and old men. Rich men and not so rich men. Saved men and lost men; yet all members of the same club.

That recent Sunday morning in San Antonio found us face to face with fellow club members. I won't share their personal Journey, but I will share what I heard them say: "This is a hard day for us", this sweet lady said. "You see, our son died on March thirteenth".

Before I really thought much about how it might sound, I blurted out; "How Funny. I'll bet you thought that we were here just for you". Please don't think me arrogant, but this is something I hear nearly every time we tell Matt's story. I continued: "The 'funny part' is that we were not here for you at all; you were here for us. Matt's day was March fifteenth". Now that I think about it. Maybe we actually were all four there for each other.

This reminded me of a great truth that is so often missed when we are consumed by our grief. Somehow we think that if God will just assuage our grief, we will respond by worshipping Him. "Do this one thing I so desperately desire God, and I will respond by saying thank you." Truth is, we must worship and thank him regardless of our circumstances or our emotions. We get things so backwards. I am not to obsess about my personal pain, but rather trust in His innate holiness. It is about *choosing* to worship.

Oh yeah, the "limited supply" thing. After an awesome lunch that Sunday, prepared by the Pastor himself, we headed back to the RV Park. As we often do, we chose the "scenic" route. This drive was a few miles further, but took us through the gorgeous Hill Country of Texas. Unless you have been there, you would not even believe this area is really in Texas. As much as I LOVE the desert portions of west Texas, I pity those who think this state is only about cactus and sagebrush. They need a good dose of some Piney Woods, a walk on the beach and a switchback laden drive to a mountain top vista, all of which can be done right here in Texas. On this day, a couple of large hills (larger than what some states call mountains) provided a wonderful opportunity for Shaunda and I to relax and talk, to debrief if you will.

As you recall from an earlier chapter, we long ago put away our posters, product bundles and even the (non-crushed velvet) tablecloth that adorned our first product table. We opted instead for the small black box, a few books and a few DVDs. We strive for understatement, to be unpretentious. As we rounded a picturesque curve I asked Shaunda if she noticed all the people walking out of the service and then walking back in. I expressed my concern that perhaps the volume was too loud. (Shaunda is the technical director you see. If it was too loud, it would have been her fault, like everything is that goes wrong if you listen to her.)

She chuckled and assured me that it was fine. "Did you see me get up and leave too?" she continued.

Actually, I hadn't. That would have likely thrown me into a public panic.

"I think the folks thought we had only the few books that were on the table. "They were going out to the lobby Joe, getting your book, and then coming back in. I had to go to the lobby and put more books out."

I guess they thought we only had a limited supply. They didn't know there was another "limited supply" nearby. How funny.

Once again I was overwhelmed by God's grace. I am grateful. And in His grace we find the only truly unlimited supply. Thank you Lord for your strength and faithfulness to me, especially in my weakness. To think that You would love me so much. So much that you would even care enough to point our truck in the direction of two people who would understand exactly how I felt that morning without me ever having to say a word.

How funny…
    How utterly amazing.

THE GREATER JOURNEY...

Read Mathew 6:5-8

In these verses, God tells us not to pray pretentious prayers, prayers that are directed to God in a superfluous way. They really aren't prayers to God at all. They are prayers intended primarily for others to hear, and perhaps cause them to think of the person praying as a pretty spiritual guy.

Real prayers contain no pretense at all. Sometimes they come from hearts so troubled that they don't even contain words (see Romans 8:26).

What is your need that is way down deep in your heart? Perhaps it is something that you long ago gave up even praying about.

Would you consider bringing it to the Lord once again? He already knows you have the need.

CHAPTER 36
"O Yes I Do"

Well, here we are once again, headed home. The first tour of YEAR TWO has taken its place squarely in the rear view. Looks like we'll be mostly working from our home base for the last half of April, May and June. We will also, however, be looking at one of our busiest times yet with short trips that include the Hill Country of Texas and three weekends in San Antonio. The book release for STORIES FROM THE ROAD is right around the corner and the accompanying music project is nearly finished, with it's release not far behind. And in between all of this, I get to help my Father in Law with a small project he's got going.

Looking back, this tour has been a real game changer for sure. We traveled thousands of miles, enjoyed the "Second Rattle Out of the Box", shared in two funerals for family members, led a Sunday Worship service, spoke three times and told Matt's story four times. It also included a real time in the "refiners fire" for me as I navigated yet another "March Madness".

On this part of the Journey I have found myself once again consistently amazed by God's flawless timing. Before I explain that further, please take a moment and read the following email I received from a dear lady. She and her husband were the focus of the "How Funny" chapter. I share it with her permission.

Joe,

Bob and I were so lifted by your message and music at our church. And, we are honored by your very kind comments that refer to us in "How Funny"! As on that special Sunday at TOBC, we felt comforted when your email came -- just as we were struggling to regain our emotional balance following our loss, we were lifted through the humor, sorrow, and hope that comes through your gifted writing talent.

We found ourselves totally exhausted following our unexpected trip to Kansas to attend the funeral services for a long time dear friend. Not sure how these losses affect you since Matt's passing, but I have to admit they take a measured emotional toll on me. I rejoice in the knowledge that he is with our Lord. (BTW, you would have loved him, and he you.) He and his wife retired as professors at Central Christian College in McPherson, where he was Dean of the English department -- a very gifted theater director and vocalist -- directing over 150 plays during his career. I know he is singing in Heaven's choir, but we do so miss him.

They had planned to escape the cold this February and come spend the entire month with us -- Our Heavenly Father had different plans. He was diagnosed with throat cancer in February. He came through all the treatments and felt the "hope", only to experience congestive heart failure. He flatlined for 10 minutes, and after 72 hours his wife prayed for him to be spared more suffering and gave him permission to go be with Jesus and their grandson who had been killed last February. Bob and I knew the pain of her decision, since we had faced this same heartache with our son, Ted. (How funny!)

Ted entered the hospital on March 1, Bob's birthday. He flatlined for 20 minutes on March 2 when they were putting him on the respirator. So, we struggled at first -- why God would give him back to us only to take him away 11 days later? I began to see God using Ted to witness from his hospital bed. Even though in ICU, Ted's doctors allowed everyone to come in to see him. Friends and leaders from different churches came to anoint him and pray with us. The waiting room was a revolving door with comforters. Ted had been at Heaven's gate twice before, and it wasn't like this. God's glory was being revealed through Ted. One friend said to me, "Myrtle, I have never been a praying

www.joeknight.us

man before, but I feel compelled to pray for your son." The day before Ted left to be with the Lord, a friend asked me, "Do you smell lilies too?" And I did, but I thought that was just to comfort me. How funny!

On this recent trip, I asked God to give us strength to be strong for our friends, especially for their daughter who is also a member of "our club". I asked Him to give us words to comfort and encourage. For the truth is, our grief is not for his passing; it is for his human absence from our lives.

I still talk to Ted each day, and sometimes I almost feel like he is still here -- and he is, through his memories that dwell in my heart! I take great comfort in that and in the knowledge we will be together again. And, I am thankful for the opportunity to share His love and grace with others; especially those who are chosen to become members of "our club".

Joe, what I didn't know until reading your book is we share another common bond, both Matt and Ted went to be with Jesus on Our Lord's Day. How funny!

May Our Lord continue to bless you and Shaunda as you continue your path to follow His sovereign will. And, someday

*may our paths again meet. Until then I
hope we can stay in touch.*

*With Christian Love,
Myrtle Parks*

Now that you have read this email in response to
Matt's story, would you agree that when hearts are
touched in such a profound way that God must be at
the center? Flawed vessel that I am, I certainly can
claim no credit. As awesome as Matt's life and
testimony were, he was just a normal kid. Besides, he
has already gone home for his reward. It has to be
God. Were we not "supposed" to be there on that
day?

Can you sense His impeccable timing yet? Perhaps
you will if I share a bit more. The Pastor of the church
where the "HOW FUNNY" event took place is a
personal friend. I merely called him a bit ahead of
when we were to be in San Antonio to see if he would
meet us for supper. When he realized we were in the
area he opened up his platform and insisted I share.
Just chance you say? Ask Bob and Myrtle Parks.
They may feel differently.

Leaving San Antonio and on the way to Houston I
learned that, through a misunderstanding, the actual
date in the Houston area would have to be
rescheduled for one week later. That was entirely
possible since the date for the following Sunday did
not work out either. That left us with another Sunday
open.

Shaunda and I got dressed, on our now unscheduled Sunday morning, and headed to a church we randomly selected from a website, mostly because they had a 10:30am start time.   The weather was especially stormy that morning making it difficult to drive.   Also, due to the fact I missed a turn, our arrival time was estimated for several minutes after their start time. Not wanting to make a "grand entrance" we turned around and headed for a church we had just passed with a start time of 10:45am.

We randomly walked in to a group of seventy-five or so folks who couldn't believe anyone would really join the "faithful few" in the midst of a tornado warning. Our presence intrigued the Pastor enough that he walked up directly to me and asked who we were and why in the world we were there.   I answered him briefly. He was so moved by just two minutes of Matt's story that shortly thereafter I was speaking and singing.

I had no books, no DVDs, no sound system, no video, no computer and no chance to prepare. To tell you the truth, I didn't even have a Bible other than my phone.   This was assuredly one of those "anytime, anywhere" opportunities.   After a few moments of sharing, the altar call was given with an amazing response. We stayed there for nearly an hour after church as literally the entire group of seventy-five worshippers lined up to shake our hands, give a hug and share with us stories of their losses.

The next weekend we rolled into our last church for this tour, the one where we had a mix-up on dates. This particular Church is like nothing we have had a part in before. They follow the "Church Under the Bridge" model. If you are not familiar with this, let me briefly explain. They literally take the Church to the streets in this large suburb of Houston Texas. Gathering in a downtown city park, they provide breakfast and lunch for the homeless. Then everyone worships together outside... outside on this absolutely perfect, beautiful sunshiny morning. Unlike last week (when I thought I should be here), we were literally worshipping just following a tornado warning.

There is more to this Church, I might add, much more, and we enjoyed a completely different, yet amazing Worship service, complete with another awesome altar call. Despite how you may feel about this type of ministry, I found myself surrounded by changed lives. This story is for another day, but I do want to share one amazing thing that happened.

On this Sunday I was the special speaker. I was to tell Matt's story on the following Wednesday night at their indoor venue. Another gentlemen joined that morning to lead worship. We had never met, yet I soon discovered that he was a very gracious gentleman, a bit younger than me.

We met under the bright sunshine to plan out the service that would start in just about an hour. Out of professional courtesy he asked for the titles of any songs I was planning to sing that morning so we didn't duplicate material. I told him I would likely do one original tune and then one worship tune that was being regularly played on pop Christian radio during this time frame. When I gave him the title, without hesitation he looked at me and recited the lyric to the second half of the third verse.

> *When a sickness takes my child away,*
> *And there's nothing I can do,*
> *My only hope is to trust You.*

"I LOVE that song", he continued, "but I just can't sing it. It's too hard for me".

"Why is it so hard for you?" I asked.

The response from this man who did not know me or had ever seen a copy of TEARS IN A BOTTLE? This man who was a total stranger no more than two minutes earlier?

"Never mind, you wouldn't understand".

Those tiny hairs on the back of your neck standing up yet? You can likely guess what the next several moments held. I won't go into detail other than to tell you that what began as a professional conversation about song selection evolved quickly into the embrace of two men who shared remarkably similar Journeys. You'd think that would be enough for one Sunday wouldn't you? Yet God stood just out of the picture waiting to dump one more huge bucket full of His unmistakable presence squarely on my head.

Both of us moved to the platform area where the sound system was now ready for use. A quick plugin and the appropriate gain and EQ settings complete, he invited me to play keys while he led worship. He started a standard strum pattern as we rehearsed his first tune. I had led this song for years and it was one on my favorites.

Amazing love, how can it be?
That You my King would die for me?
Amazing love, I know its true.
And it's my joy to honor You,
In all I do, I honor You.

Then he asked if I knew this tune as he started a different strum pattern and chord progression in a new key. I recognized the song immediately. For those who have followed Matt's story I likely don't have to even tell you the song title.   As he began to sing the hair stood up on the back of *my* neck as the tears welled up in my eyes.

The splendor of a King,
Clothed in majesty,
Let all the world rejoice.

This man sang strong and confident, but it was not his voice that I heard.

Success to some may be defined as practicing their craft in a huge venue surrounded by thousands of screaming fans.   While there is nothing inherently wrong with this, on this Sunday, God chose for me to tell my story "under the bridge".   I would not trade venues.   His perfect timing placed me where He was without any doubt closer than any brother could ever be. You see, this is not about me, it never has been. It's not even about Matt.   This Journey is about God. Our small part is found in our choice to worship Him regardless of life's circumstances; following the example that Matt left behind for us to follow.

Today I still remember one particular Sunday as the countdown clock on the big screens clicked down to service start time. I picture Matt sitting on the stairs leading to the Worship center, guitar between his legs, his entire body raising and lowering with every breath. I looked on the visage of a young man that somehow seemed to resemble my son less and less every week. Face and body swelled from all the steroids, ruddy complexion, and thick, dark hair long gone.

I still remember telling him that he "didn't have to go on" that day. And I still remember the four words he rather defiantly said back to me: "O YES I DO."

Matt understood, even at his young age, that the ability to weather life's storms and the willingness to worship in spite of them were inexorably linked. Dealing with the difficulties of our Journey is made immeasurably easier by a simple refusal to hate God, replaced instead by a dogged determination to proclaim as Job did..."Though He slay me, I will trust in Him".

I still have no inclination of what the future holds for KNIGHTsong Ministries beyond YEAR TWO. I have no idea if I will even be alive then. I'm not certain there will even be a "world as we know it" by the time YEAR THREE rolls around. Perhaps before then we will hear the amazing sound of a trumpet and the shout of an angel fill the air. I'm good with that for sure.

Yet for now, do I really believe that God can work out even the tiniest details of our life? O yes I do. I also believe that whatever comes around the next corner, He's already got it covered. He has incredible timing. He is never merely on time. He is always several steps ahead. I'm certainly not the first to have arrived at such a conclusion. I'll close with these words from a very old song; a song that is as fresh to me this moment as if Ira had just been penned the words...

Many things about tomorrow,
I don't seem to understand,
But I know who holds tomorrow,
And I know who holds my hand.

Words and Music by Ira Stanphill
© 1950, renewal 1977 By Sinspiration/ASCAP

CHAPTER 37
Tomorrow's Troubles

It is still the wee hours of the morning. The enveloping darkness of the night has yet to surrender its control over our world to the unyielding demands of a rising sun. Soon the dozens of birds that now sit quietly will sing to welcome first light. Then the neighbor's roosters will assure that everyone within earshot understands that it is time to face another day. For now, however, I am alone in the quiet with only my thoughts to keep me company.

For me, being at our home base is not really that different, and then again it is. This back corner of my father-in-law's property that you read about early in the Journey has been transformed into one of the nicest RV parks we have visited, thanks in no small part to my mother-in-law's green thumb. What began as an empty field now boasts full hookups, a gravel pad and RV barn and a landscaped patio situated just to the right of a small pond full of fish. Soon the fish will start their morning feeding ritual, which I have come to interpret as merely an attempt to get my attention.

Being home is not really that different. We have spent the last several weekends at Churches within driving distance. We have shared Matt's story twice and helped with the music at a third opportunity. That opportunity was with a smaller church just under a hundred miles away. This is one of the few churches I have asked to partner with us at a much deeper level. As such, we get back there every opportunity we can, and they reward us with some of the richest friendships we could ever dream of.

This group has welcomed us to join in their regularly scheduled fellowship times and even create similar opportunities when we are in the area. Simple, beautiful opportunities like the recent pot luck/Texas BBQ dinner where several couples shared a beautiful evening by the lake. Soon I found myself around the dining room table with just the men involved in a deep discussion. A discussion that ended with their desire to find out how they could best pray for us. These are folks who are engaged to the point that they seem to want to know every little detail of our Journey. They ask us questions. They make us feel valued. I am convinced that they genuinely care about each heartache and each success just as if they were a part of both. Come to think of it, I guess they really are just as much a part of both as we are.

The most recent telling of Matt's story was accompanied by what we have almost come to expect at the conclusion of the presentation; people who are willing to stay for long periods of time to share their hugs, and to share their stories. Both of these churches were of the larger variety, so these lines were long. Some waited for nearly an hour. Talk about surreal.

I won't share their stories for a couple of reasons. First, because these are their stories and not mine to tell. Second, because some may read this and think that the retelling seems a bit self-serving. I assure you that it would not be. It is unbelievably humbling to be presented by God with a story that so deeply moves people. I sense an overwhelming responsibility to use this gift wisely. I will tell you that I heard things in the past weeks that on one occasion required that I excuse myself from the line for a moment. I headed for the first vacant Sunday School classroom I could find. I had to pour my heart out to God for just a moment thanking Him for using such an unworthy vessel to carry His message of unbelievable hope to this world.

As I entered the Sanctuary at the second opportunity to tell Matt's story, a lady greeted me. My initial thought was that she looked somewhat familiar. "Are you the Joe Knight that sang with the Emmanuels?" she asked. And in a few seconds more than forty years and thousands of miles had flown together into one place. She and her husband had pastored a Church that hosted my group when I was a teenager. The really amazing part? All those years ago I was based in Ohio. I sang for her and her husband in Nebraska. On this Sunday we would become reacquainted in Texas. If no one is going to say it for me, I guess I just have to use one of the most overworked expressions of all time myself. Sure is a small world.

As you might guess, on that evening there just wasn't enough time after church. She and her good friend waited around until the last person was through and all my equipment was loaded. This reunion demanded to be continued over ice cream. Soon we would share our stories of loss. Mine, of my son. Her's and her friend's? They were both wonderful Pastor's wives, who had recently said goodbye to faithful lifelong ministry partners.

You see; being home is not really that different. And then again it is.

This is Memorial Day weekend. Yesterday I had nowhere in particular to sing, so we had the opportunity to be in services where I had served the twenty-one years before beginning this Journey of a Lifetime. Talk about some crazy mixed up emotions. This is a strange point in the Journey for me. In some ways, it is more difficult to be at home in Texas than anywhere else. We entered the sanctuary unannounced and sat in the back; I mean the very back. I am quite sure we took someone else's seat. Those back seats in a church always come at a premium.

We had not been in services since November. It was good to go back. It was hard to go back. I could not tell you how my heart was squeezed when a line again formed after services. Many people that I have spent so much of my life with came by to share hugs, and tears, and stories. Seems like after some time had passed since we left, certain folks will take the opportunity to tell you what you meant to them. And so I found myself in the back row, nowhere near a convenient Sunday School room where I could run and hide, even if for just a moment.

Please read this next part carefully. I don't want to be misunderstood. I really wanted to leave my church and go out to tell Matt's story. I also didn't want to leave my church at all. Does that make any sense to you? I'll be quite honest, I read it again and I'm not sure I fully understand what it means.

Again, please don't think I am feeling sorry for myself in any way. It's just that in some ways making the decision to set out on this Journey was the first time I have lived by faith in many years, at least in a financial aspect. I did not earn an exorbitant salary at my church by any means. Many in similar positions as mine earn much more. Many earn much less. I was somewhere in the middle, yet it was comfortable. We lived in a nice home in a decent neighborhood. Our home was smaller than many and larger than some. In was not in the "best' location, but not the worst either. We were quite content however, living where we were, ministering where we were.

And then I made the choice to pursue this ministry. And then everything changed.

I must admit that recently I have found myself worried about the future. I'm not talking about this year, or next, or even the next or the next. I am worried that I might find myself one day living in a dilapidated fifth wheel, worried about how I will provide for my wife. There. When you see this thought process staring back at you in print, it is quite ugly.

Being at services today was a reminder of the financial stability I left behind.

I guess I am consumed with tomorrow's troubles.

And I guess its time to relearn another lesson that I thought I put to bed years ago. Seems I remember Jesus Himself standing on the side of a mountain addressing just such a human perspective, and then obliterating it completely.

He told us not to be worried about tomorrow. Tomorrow will take care of itself. We are to seek the things of God today and trust Him to take care of tomorrow's troubles. We are not to even consider tomorrow. Seems, as well, that I learned this same lesson sitting at the foot of a hospital bed in the wee hours of another early morning so many years ago. I learned then to hold on to today, or better yet this very moment. How quickly the sands slip through the hourglass, and they are forever gone.

How foolish to allow tomorrow's troubles to steal today's joy.

At least I thought I learned all of this. Another generation of readers might not understand the following at all, but for toady, I guess my life should use the hashtag #stilllearning.

It is true that when I walked into my church today, I sat in the back instead of standing on the platform. It is true that as I write these words, another family sleeps inside the walls I used to call "home". It is true that I no longer have the unspeakable blessing of being a Pastor to so many people, many whose day-to-day lives I still deeply care about today.

It is also true that in the last year I have shared Matt's story with thousands of people who would have otherwise never heard of his great faith. Many of these people are now new friends who pray for us. I was reminded yesterday that many of our old friends still do as well. I have witnessed people accept Christ and have seen others literally run home into his loving arms. I have heard a hundred stories of loss and been told as many times how impactful our message of hope has been in their lives.

I have travelled the freeways and back roads of this beautiful nation. I have summited a mountain and held two beautiful grandchildren in my arms within moments of when they breathed their first breath. I have reconnected with dozens of old friends. I have stared into a night sky that held a million points of light and taken in the sunrise as it woke up that same night sky. I have walked along the seashore watching the same sun rise over the watery horizon and at the same time held tightly to the hand of one of the greatest gifts God ever gave a broken heart.

And I have felt the loving arms of a Savior wrap me up so tightly that I was protected against any foe that dare approach such a powerful refuge.

How dare I worry about tomorrow's trouble?

Instead, I choose today's joy.

Funny, I can hear birds singing now and the horizon now has taken on a familiar glow casting its light on this small corner of the world. Seems like I remember something about another sunrise at an earlier time.

The same lesson that was true then is true today. He is still big enough for my questions.

Maybe this morning I wasn't alone with my thoughts after all.

Maybe I never am.

THE GREATER JOURNEY...

Read Matthew 6:25,26

In verse 26, what things are we not supposed to worry about? Do any of your worries fall into any of these categories?

In verse 26, what does Jesus tell us to consider in order to confront the source of our worries?

Can you think of another time when Jesus suggested we consider something else as well? (Read Luke 22:12-30)

What is the underlying source of worry? Need a hint? It's one of the three purposes for THE GREATER JOURNEY Live Worship Event. Need another? Read Proverbs 3:5, 6.

Chapter 38
Spot On

Don't you hate those ridiculous wooden signs that bear those silly left brained platitudes? You know what I mean. Those plaques designed to completely take over a wall in your home. They contain trite sayings that cause my wife to tear up, and make me want to tear them up. One word describes them all: drivel. You know, sayings like "Life is not made up of years, it is made up of moments" and "I Love You to the Moon and Back".

Working from our home base for several weeks assures us some interesting weekend trips. In less than a month, we head out for the last tour of this Journey of a Lifetime. Hard to believe it's gone by so quickly. This particular "weekend trip" actually covers ten days and includes two weekends. We are returning to a Church a few hours away to do two consecutive weekends of interim work. We are scheduled for the week in between to begin some remote recording work nearer home on a music project for some dear friends.

These first few days at home have been a wonderful experience even before we even pulled the sound system out of the truck. The proximity of this mini-trip created an opportunity to add Makenna, our nine-year-old granddaughter, to the mix for the first few days. That addition assures several thousand variances from a normal weekend. Variances like a thousand added giggles, a hundred questions, and the fact that I heard the word "Poppi" at least a million times. Not to mention eating at certain fast food restaurants that we typically avoid at all costs.

A day spent in downtown San Antonio Texas yielded the most awesome video of our Journey yet. Seems that you couldn't see the hidden camera behind the mirror while you were asked to touch the end of your nose with your tongue. I'm glad I don't act silly around my Granddaughter like Shaunda does. I'm also glad she didn't have her phone handy when Cowboy Bob and his faithful steed danced playfully around the pool while singing "Happy trails to you". Both of these momentous events brought about more than a few of those thousands of giggles. I'm afraid I'll have to admit that they weren't all Makenna's.

One really crazy thing about time spent invested with grandchildren is how somehow these moments bring with them pieces of long ago forgotten memories. This was assuredly true for me during this weekend. Maybe it was the 1980's era fashion dolls that once found their home in my daughter's toy box. On this trip they found their way to the small tub of toys that made it into Makenna's back seat kingdom. Or it might have been the fact that within three minutes of arriving at the motel Makenna had already changed into her swimsuit, much like another small child might have done some fifty years earlier.

I know for sure I heard Matt whispering over and over in my ear, "Never take one moment of life for granted. Never take one moment of life for granted". I have no idea what today holds for you, but I would encourage you to look for the moments, and listen for his message.

You know what the really interesting thing is? I'm afraid I must admit that those silly sayings are, well... spot on.

THE GREATER JOURNEY...

Read Ephesians 5:15, 16

Why not ask God to help you slow down today? Don't take one moment of today for granted. Remember, there are no assurances for tomorrow. We may never pass this way again.

Take a look at James 4:14.

Part 5
Changing Seasons

CHAPTER 39
All In

Sometimes you've just got to play the cards that you are dealt. Other times you can take the ones you have and just bluff your way through. You can follow standard advice and lead with your highest card only to encounter disaster when someone else plays a trump. There are days when you find that no matter how hard you try, you seem to discover the reality that someone else in the game is holding all the aces. That's just the luck of the draw. That's also when its most important to not over bet your chips. You've got to know when to hold 'em, and know when to... never mind. Even I won't go there. There are a few crucial times however, every once in a while, when you just have to go "all in".

While others have chosen a game of cards to represent the Journey that is our lives, I have chosen in this work to use a road trip to represent the same. I thought I would give you a break from all the travel analogies for a few moments and try out the card thing. I'll be quick though. I remember dozens of sermons through the years espousing the evils of playing cards. We may need to tell our story in some of their churches. I hope they know I'm only playing the joker here. (That was the last one, I promise.)

We have all sat in front of our televisions and bore witness as a drama ascends to a climax when the old west gamblers carefully eye each other up. Everyone in the quintessential western saloon focuses his attention on the main table where a game of poker is nearing its conclusion. Cowboys lean back in creaking wooden chairs while closely eyeing their fellow gamesmen, hoping to pick up on a revealing tell. The music typically employs a corresponding crescendo. Only then does the hero (or villain, depending on the storyline) place both hands squarely behind all his chips. Timed with the final musical emphasis, he shoves all his chips to the center of the table. Just as the music stops he confidently announces: "I'm all in".

In the pursuit of transparency, I must admit that with regard to my future plans, I have been hedging my bets a bit. (Sorry, that one just snuck in.) I kept back the idea that I might re-enter Law Enforcement at some point. I have kept up with all the appropriate CE units, firearms and mandatory training to keep my state license intact. I also thought I might one day be able to secure a church ministry position, even after realizing that the "skinny jean" thing might be a glaring issue.

Meanwhile, back at the saloon.

This is the moment of truth. No longer is it that just a few dollars are on the table. Everything is on the line. Sometimes it included the gamblers pocket watch (complete with his wife's picture) or maybe even his horse and saddle. What comes next determines the final resolution to the story. With anticipation now at a fevered pitch, it happens: a commercial for a toilet bowl cleanser. We find ourselves caught in the unforgiving clutches of a cliffhanger tantamount to the burning question that lasted the entirety of one summer in the distant past: Who shot JR? As I've said before, ask someone over fifty. They'll explain that one to you.

We have enjoyed these few weeks working out of our home base. These have included several presentations of Matt's story, culminating with an unbelievable month of June. Yet for us, the close of this incredible Journey is now in view, the two years nearly at its conclusion. The future, now a rather immediate future, remains gray. I have sent out no resumes or talked with any Pastors pursuant to employment. I have processed the appropriate paperwork with reference to my Law Enforcement retirement. When we start the truck, hook up "The Virge" and join hands for prayer, Shaunda and I will be leaving clean. We have chosen to go "all in" if you will.

Can I be dreadfully honest here? As I mentioned earlier, I must admit that even though I have spent the majority of my lifetime in vocational ministry, it has been quite a while since I have really "lived by faith" in the simpler sense.

Now please don't misunderstand, years ago I learned to depend on God for the genuine success of every area of my ministry. As a musician, I can produce pretty good music without any supernatural help from God at all. I hope that didn't shock you too much or seem in any way arrogant. Its just that God has gifted me with a specific skill set that makes it possible to accomplish certain musical goals. Here's the rub though, great music has never changed anyone's eternity. Great music does little to turn a ministry team into a "family' and keep it intact for more than twenty years. While human effort can produce a slick presentation and the appearance of Godliness, genuine and lasting value in ministry is simply impossible to achieve without the presence and power of the Holy Spirit. In that aspect, I have learned to live totally dependent on Him and His power.

On the other hand, I have had the privilege of working in more than one church that experienced no financial difficulties. As I think about it now, I never one time in thirty-five years of ministry found myself wondering if my paycheck was in jeopardy. I have never been "let go" from a position, and only once went unemployed in my adult life. That was only for a few weeks, and was entirely of my own volition.

This Journey however, is an honest experiment in the "living by faith" thing. I can tell you unequivocally that this piece of the puzzle is one factor that has provided so much refreshment. Watching God regularly perform "little miracles" has been an adventure. A look in the rear view mirror if you will, selling the family home and nearly all of our "stuff" turned out to not really be much of a sacrifice at all. From today's perspective, our headlong rush into a minimalistic lifestyle proved to be, for me, one of the most freeing experiences of my entire life. For the record, I highly recommend the "living by faith" scene.

While ours is certainly no "cliffhanger" compared to the gambler, a final dramatic curve in the road awaits on our JOURNEY OF A LIFETIME. (Wow, sure feels good to leave the card table and get back behind the windshield.) This final tour begins in a few short days. It is scheduled to last several months and cover the remainder of the summer, and most of the fall for that matter, hence the name of the tour: Changing Seasons. As you might readily guess, just as with the JOURNEY OF A LIFETIME, there is a double meaning in that title as well.

Still well short of a "cliffhanger", this does leave a rather burning question yet unanswered (at least for me). "Will there be a YEAR 3?" While I genuinely do not have a definitive answer as of yet, I am beginning to sense that God may be doing something special here. And just like He loves to do, it likely will not be something easily seen. It seems rather to be a significant shift in my internal perspective.

So after several reflective, refreshing days, the calendar points to the beginning of this final adventure. Not sure what to expect for next year, but as far as this Journey is concerned, we are no longer at the end of the beginning, but rather the beginning of the end.

These last few days held some unbelievable moments spent with friends and family, and even more manifestations of the grace of God. They continued right through our final service when I spoke briefly afterwards to yet another mom; a mom who sadly was a member of our club. I heard her words. My heart bowed in humility when she told me how God had used Matt's story to touch her life. She told me that she finally realized that her struggles with the loss of her son were ultimately brought about by her choice to not forgive God, and how she had realized that it was indeed possible to make a different choice.

With the successful release of STORIES FROM THE ROAD, we were likewise blessed financially as well. Several folks shared as God led them, but none moved me more that the letter that came in the mail just today. This message, written in handwriting that was difficult to read, was accompanied by an explanation. It was a physical condition that brought about the difficulty. The note of appreciation was moving. The few dollars represented by the enclosed check was a gift equal to any gift given regardless of amount. I found myself grateful, very humbled and once again convinced that God has indeed blessed us with a valid ministry.

While "enjoying" these last few days at our home base, I must admit that my heart is already somewhere out there on the road. Seems that this crazy lifestyle seems to "fit me right down to the ground". What I learned early in my ministry years remains an immutable fact. We must have God's blessing to enjoy genuine ministry success. With eyes now fixed on the view through the windshield, I need your prayers more than ever as I find myself "all in".

THE GREATER JOURNEY...

So what really is faith? (See Hebrews 11:1)

Ready for a really lengthy bible study? Here we go! Take out a pen and paper and make a list of the bible characters listed in the following passage. Use your concordance or favorite bible search engine and discover the story behind each name. Then you might grasp the significance of the value of faith in our lives.

Now grab that pen and read the entirety of Hebrews 11.

CHAPTER 40
What Year Is It?

"Do you know what year it is?"

That is one of the standardized questions I used many times in Law Enforcement when doing field interviews. Whenever I might happen upon someone who seemed disconnected or perhaps impaired, it is vital to first determine if that person has a grasp on some basic realities. Are they in command of where they are, who they are and what is going on around them? Hence the question. I would also ask if they knew who was president. That question was occasionally answered like this: "Yeah, I know. Me. I am the President (or God, or Jesus Christ)". While not the correct answer, it certainly gives the answer to the deeper question I was really asking.

 The "Changing Seasons" tour is off and running, but I'll be honest. I haven't noticed any changes in the season just yet. It's

just hot, well perhaps a different form of hot. Add a large dose of humidity to your definition of hot and you'll be close. This particular morning finds us on the Georgia coast. No mountains or rivers to look at from my window today. Why I can't even see the ocean from here. But I can tell you that our more than one hundred foot long campsite is surrounded by palm trees and towering oaks, with branches intertwined, so as to allow rays of sunshine through the canopy highlighting the flowing moss and climbing vines. Not so bad.

Sometimes it seems that God's blessings are like a cup of cool water poured over my head on a hot day like today. I love the way it refreshes and cools, wiping away fatigue and clearing the mind. Then there are other times that it seems as if a bucket has replaced the cup. Of late, it seems more like a steady shower. I have no idea why God allows the journey of our lives to ebb and flow the way He does. Periods of brilliant sunshine followed by periods of refreshing rain. Perhaps it is because if we always enjoyed the "buckets of blessing" our spirits might not long as much for the tender embrace and open arms waiting us at the end of our Journey.

I would not dare minimize the blessings of the public opportunities to tell Matt's story. Once again this past weekend we basked in the powerful presence of the Holy Spirit moving though the worship center, touching lives in ways I only once could have dreamed of. One more time I stood back and marveled as Shaunda shared one on one with yet another mom; and gave away yet another book. The first few weeks of this tour however, held equal blessing in more private settings. Once again I was reminded that prayers can be voiced and worship can take place in groups of four and five. As a matter of fact, seems I remember reading somewhere about a supernaturally powerful Presence in the middle of just two or three.

It began with an entire day spent on the beach with a friend who is a Pastor. (Note please, that the syntax is chosen intentionally. This is entirely different than a "Pastor friend".) It was just a coincidence that before we left on this tour he had the need of a fill in Worship Leader on the one Sunday I had open. It was merely by chance that we discovered he would be vacationing less than thirty miles from where we were planning to be. It was only happenstance that the four of us would end up together for an entire afternoon and evening. It was only a fluke that the backdrop of the gulf waves framed wonderful conversation that would soon turn to family and ministry and... well, then again, maybe it wasn't by coincidence, chance, happenstance or a fluke at all.

Soon we were headed to Atlanta. A Friday dinner and early setup would leave Saturday lunch open for a very special opportunity. Way back when Shaunda and I were first married (way, way back), there was an older couple at our Church. They were an unlikely pair to befriend us, and yet they made the choice to do just that. We were guests in their home on several occasions. Their homestead boasted three overstocked ponds that in turn offered a great location to take my three boys fishing, and to take Joey for some much needed time alone well before I added the "s" to "boy". Every so often they would suggest that we all go out to dinner. This older couple made certain that each visit included a time of encouragement for our family, and an opportunity to talk about our struggles. Soon we would finish the meal and they would always insist on covering the check.

Saturday morning found us knocking on a brand new door to visit these great old friends. Now well into their nineties, they had just celebrated sixty eight years of marriage. (Wow... sixty-eight years!) I don't believe that the few hours we spent together ever lacked for conversation. As a matter of fact, there were usually two conversations going at the same time. Sometimes three. We shared current events, new dreams and old memories. Every so often it seemed we had to take a break, shed some tears and some private moments of gratitude, and then get right back at it. It is such a blessing to enjoy unexpected moments, to share in the common bond of Christ, and to say "thank you" one more time.

Too soon it was out the door and to their favorite "mom and pop" lunch spot. Although we tried to persuade them before, during and after the meal, I quickly realized I would have had to literally wrestle this gentleman to the ground for the check. For those of you who know these great folks, you will understand this next statement. I really think I might have been able to whoop Jack, but I would not even consider taking on Jimmie for one moment! Oh yeah, in case I failed to say it enough on Saturday, thank you for being there for me, over and over when I needed you so much.

At the close of this chapter you will see a picture of three strange looking young guys. When I look at them now, I see mere children; boyish faces and innocent smiles. The "boys" in the middle and on the right you may not recognize. The one on the left only vaguely resembles a guy we all know. The occasion? The day I moved from my first full time church position that I held after my home church. It was a cold Ohio evening after a long day of loading a rented moving truck, and it marked the end of an equally cold season in my life. I had resigned a successful ministry position because I was put in the situation where cashing my paycheck would have forced me into collusion in an illegal financial dealing made by the person in authority over me. The months leading up to this evening were stressful to the point where I had ended up in the hospital for a week. The date? 1984... and not the Orwellian book.

Now, back to the story. A time of fellowship with one of the "boys" after that recent Friday setup soon found a printed copy of this picture introduced to the conversation to the chagrin of both of us. I was the boy on the left. He was the boy in the middle. I worked on staff with these men in that highly stressful environment. Our JOURNEY OF A LIFETIME provided for us an opportunity to see each other once again. No longer boys for sure, he is a decade older than me, at least for two more weeks, when I will join him in his decade.

The interim years with their accompanying geographical distances provided little opportunity for us to interact. No exaggeration here, within thirty seconds we were both "boys" again. Shared memories sparked long forgotten other memories. My Journey has held a couple of trips through the cornfield. His had as well. We discovered that our first "cornfield experiences" were eerily similar. The next day, on that Saturday evening we stopped by their home once again. After a dozen or so more stories and a thousand laughs we sat down over some thick steaks he had just grilled.

Between conversations and without even thinking, I blurted out. Is this 2017 or 1981? (Actually it would have been 1984). Odd, but had an interviewing Police Officer asked me that moment the question: "What Year is it?" I feared I would have been considered impaired at worst, disconnected at best. Truth is, I was more connected than I had been before this weekend. It's just that in many ways, time had been strangely washed away.

Now add to this the awesome support of friends and family before we left and the amazing Sunday service that was to follow, you can see why this weekend was so extraordinary.

That middle boy? Despite the best efforts of the adversary, he continues on into the ministry into his next decade. He serves as Worship Leader in the Church where we would tell Matt's story.

The boy on the right? After enduring the same storm as I did all those years ago, He started a new Church in another town. He still serves that Church as Pastor to this day. Lord willing, I will see him in a few weeks.

The boy on the left? He will soon share his friend's decade and only by the grace of God continues in the ministry today.

One more thing that all these stories share is that they all ended with a "goodbye". We said "goodbye" to all our friends and family before pulling out on this tour. After a great day on the beach I said "goodbye" to my friend who is a Pastor. After Saturday's lunch, with a hug, a prayer and many tears I said "goodbye" to Jack and Jimmie. After a great lunch following Sunday's service, I said "goodbye" to the boy in the middle and his family.

Funny how on one hand I can fully enjoy this Journey of our lifetimes, and at the exact same moment long to be somewhere else. Somewhere else where it will never again matter what year it is. A "somewhere else" where we can all be together at exactly the same time; a somewhere where we'll never have to say "goodbye".

THE GREATER JOURNEY...

Is heaven real to you?
What does it mean to you?
Know anyone already there?
Want to go there one day?

Want a little reminder of what it will be like? Try reading these verses.

Revelation 21:1-4   John 14:1-3

CHAPTER 41
The Journey Of A Lifetime

So is a picture really worth a thousand words? I hope so, and please don't panic. I think I can say everything that is on my heart this morning in well under a thousand words.

An opportunity for some down time in southeastern Georgia provided some amazing views and some unbelievable history. It is quite sobering indeed to literally stand on the dock at the exact same location where men, women and children were offloaded from the cargo holds of ships where they had been held captive, only to be auctioned off as nothing more than a commodity.

And at the other extreme, and on the very next day, I ran through a tunnel of moss-covered trees. In the back of my mind I heard those fateful words: "Run, Forrest, Run!" I shot some video during our first year at the exact spot where Forrest decided it was time to stop running. It seemed only right to shoot some more at the exact spot where he started. And yes there is an edited version of that one.

Two facts to consider at this point: Forrest Gump never really existed, and you will never see the video. How about a third fact? While Forrest never was a real person, with real dreams and a real family, the human beings who stood at the same place on the dock where I would stand so many years later, were.

How about I share a few stories from recent amazing Live Worship Events where we told the story of Matt's life? I could start by telling you about the unspeakable power of the Holy Spirit. I have spoken many times over the years in Church services and secular public settings. I know what it feels like to hear your words bounce back off the back wall. I have known the inner struggle when I sensed that the worshippers were not engaged, or worse yet, were listening with contempt. I also know what it is like when it seems as if every single word is slicing cleanly through a carefully guarded façade. I can accomplish those first scenarios with zero supernatural intervention. The last one is totally impossible without it.

At one point in THE GREATER JOURNEY Live Worship Event, I challenge people to worship regardless of whether their Journey has them currently on a mountaintop or in a valley. I tell how Matt accomplished this with these four words" "O yes I do". I ask them to genuinely worship in spite of any struggles. I could tell you about the service where the worshipper's response was a combination of tears, shouts and a thunderous applause that lasted so long it threw off the timing for the next song.

And then there was the service where the Pastor asked me to stand at the front with him during the invitation; wow, didn't see that one coming. "If you're here", he explained, "And you are struggling with grief, why not come and Joe will pray with you". And man did I hear the stories. Car accidents, illness, children taken by cancer and the ever-present elderly mother who no one in the church had known that she lost a child decades earlier. During all this the Church Worship Team of this great church sang, and those in the room sang, and we all cried and worshipped. And after a lengthy time of invitation for hurting people, the Pastor extended an invitation for those who did not know Christ to simply trust Him as Savior, and many did.

Oddly enough, it seemed to me that in the midst of this glorious worship experience I noticed, at least in my mind, a young man standing in the back of the room. He was a shorter guy with a tightly shaved beard and moustache. His arms were folded and from his face burst an irrepressible smile. He was dressed in shorts, t-shirt and; flip-flops, guitar slung over his shoulder. Though no one else could see him or even sensed he was there, I did. As a matter of fact, he's never really that far away. I think he was pleased at what was happening all around him. He should be. If not for his life, and death, none of this would be happening at all.

I could tell you of another service that was nearly exactly like this one. I could point out that here I enjoyed the presence of another special guest. It was a musketeer. A man who had planned his vacation around this service and had driven halfway across the United States with three family members to be there that day.

Then I could tell you about the time we planned to have lunch with the Pastor after the service. Instead, we had the privilege of dining with a couple that we had never met. When we had spoken only a few words, it was obvious that we had much in common. They have shared a similar Journey. The unthinkable had happened at their house. They were members of our club.

Then there was the service where I met an amazing young lady. She was a Pastor's wife. She was the mother of two small children, a little boy and a little girl. When we prayed together, she was but two weeks short of the first anniversary of the loss of her husband. She was amazing all right. Her tears were not even for herself that morning, but rather for her children.

And I could go on…and on…and on.

But what if I told you that all of these services really happened the same day? All of this occurred in the space of one week, culminating with back-to-back services at aa single Church in Statesboro, GA.

Please don't misunderstand. I do not boast of anything, except for God Himself. He is the only One capable of such miracles. I just want to remind you, and me, why this has been the Journey of a Lifetime.

I have to stop now. I just checked the word count... 1007. Guess I couldn't accomplish it after all.

THE GREATER JOURNEY...

Please consider the following verses:
1 Corinthians 1:31   2 Corinthians 10:17
2 Corinthians 12:9   Galatians 6:14
2 Thessalonians 1:4

Is it ok to boast about certain things?
If so, then what?

CHAPTER 42
A Thousand Words...

Let's try out that "thousand word" thing with just a few pictures, shall we?

Smokey Mountain National Park

Black Canyon of the Gunnison National Park

Shaunda at the Horseshoe, Utah

Monument Valley, Utah

Sunset at Big Bend National Park

K_S

Sunset at Mill Creek, Ohio

RV Park in Moab, Utah

Moab, Utah

Bryce Canyon National Park, Utah

Zion National Park, Utah

Alpenglow, Crested Butte, Colorado

Sunrise On The Beach, Galveston, TX

The View From My Window, Smoky Mountain National Park

Where Do We Go From Here? Knoxville, TN

CHAPTER 43
Hallowed Ground

Throughout history our lifetimes have been characterized in different ways. They have been considered as "pages in a book" or the "seasons of our lives" as compared to the seasons of a calendar year. Troubled times have been described as valleys, while joyous ones pictured as mountaintops. A brand new day has been considered as a "fresh canvas", while the final moments of our lives have been compared to the hands on a clock approaching midnight. The apostle Paul presented life as a race, one where the runner should pace himself through patience, and where the end of our lives is celebrated by receiving that crown of glory at the finish line.

As for me, I have always loved family vacations. I wrote about this rather extensively in STORIES FROM THE ROAD. I guess that's what made it very easy for me to think of my lifetime in those terms, that of a Journey, from the cradle to the grave. I've used more than a few of these metaphors in the pages of my books.

You see, in the most practical terms, this has truly been the "Journey of a Lifetime" for us. To this point we have driven more than 73,000 miles. We have literally enjoyed a lifetime of vacations while at the same time telling Matt's story to more than ten thousand people who had never heard it before. And there are adventures yet planned as we finish the final weeks of this two-year Journey. Tomorrow holds a whitewater-rafting trip and right around the corner (see, there's one of those metaphors right there) is a planned ten-day road trip through Canada and New England.

Between now and the actual end of the two years we have scheduled another twenty opportunities to tell Matt's Story. On one hand I find myself in discussions concerning a second edition and distribution of TEARS IN A BOTTLE on a scale I never once even dreamed about. On the other hand, I am in discussions about telling Matt's story in partnership with a ministry who holds meetings all across the nation for mothers who have lost children. When this dream began years before I ever left my Church, who could have ever imagined we would be here today? Not me, that's for sure. I was then, and still am, enjoying the Journey one day at a time. That's all my little brain can handle. Actually, that's what I have chosen to do. Another lesson brought home by Matt.

This morning we were driving from our Nations capital northbound on US 15. I was captivated by the fact that nearly every town we passed through had a name familiar to me. I had read of the tragedies that occurred there, as each was a location of a conflict in our Country's civil war. This truly is, as Abraham Lincoln described it, hallowed ground.

Then we turned westbound on Interstate 70. My thoughts instantly changed as I was keenly aware of a strange feeling. I soon realized that I was having one of those "seems like I've been here before" moments.

Shaunda had just pulled "The Virge" into a beautiful rest area located in the mountains of Maryland. The buildings were new, but the interstate had been there for many years. Then something occurred to me. When I was a small boy, a familiar beach on the Atlantic Ocean in Maryland was the family summer vacation spot for several consecutive years. There was an inexpensive motel, adorned with a conspicuous mermaid figure, that was situated a few blocks from the beach. That coupled with the fact that this was only a days drive from where I was raised, made for the perfect vacation getaway. And the highway? This same Interstate. The direct route from my parent's home to the ocean. I *had* been here before.

And then two more threads of my life came together. This "Journey of a Lifetime" is in actuality for me the Journey of *my* Lifetime. Likely fifty years had passed since I stood on that same ground in Maryland. Instead of hopping out of the cab of a diesel pickup, I could have just as easily have been crawling out of the back seat of a two-door 1960 Ford Custom. I wonder if that's a small piece of what heaven might be like? Or even God, for that matter. The same Yesterday, Today and Forever. Hallowed ground.

CHAPTER 44
We'll Leave The Lights On

Driving home from West Texas to East Texas on one of the last trips of this JOURNEY OF A LIFETIME, Shaunda and I had a lot of time to talk. It is now 2017, more than 8½ years since Matt passed away. As we talked we came to realize that other than his close family, Matt would likely have been talked about, and thought about for that matter very little on this day. His ministry would certainly have long ago come to an end. And that's only right for sure. But because we have been allowed by God to take this unbelievable Journey, his story of great faith lives on.

On this particular Sunday service we had just completed, if not for this great privilege, Matt's influence would have been non-existent, his ministry effectively over. Instead, on this very day many people were touched by his story. As a matter of fact, over this two-year Journey more than ten thousand people have heard of his deliberate choice to worship God in the darkest of days, and thousands more have read of it in TEARS IN A BOTTLE. To have a small part in this endeavor is one of the greatest blessings of our lives.

And...

...just that quick, this two year JOURNEY OF A LIFETIME draws to a close. Although I knew it would be this way, it still seems unbelievable how quickly these two years have passed. I guess, truth be told, all of my life has been that way as well. While still in Bible College I recall how the news media was filled with the biggest story of 1976. I still remember when all those around me were celebrating the same event, the bicentennial of our nation.

Even then we were all talking about what life would be like when we bravely faced a brand new century. It was only the blink of an eye until I was on patrol that night when the millennium came to a close. I was there with what seemed like every other police officer in the world on that very night. Y2K, the night we faced midnight with a bit of trepidation, wondering what the world's computers might do. Pity anyone who committed a minor violation that night. Any Officer making a traffic stop was guaranteed at least three cover units. There was for once "lots of us" and "few of them" as everyone stayed home and waited for, well, as it came about, waited for nothing to happen. And as I write these words, I realize that all of that was now nearly twenty years ago.

As the relentless pace of time continues unabated I realize once again that I am no longer a young man. Most of the time, these days, my mind and my spirit tell me otherwise. Not to worry though, my body is always there to remind me of the truth. And speaking of being reminded, I now remember that these two years have indeed been a Journey of a Lifetime, a gift from God to see things and do things I might never have otherwise seen or done. More importantly I have had an even greater opportunity to learn things I might never have learned.

The Journey of our Lifetime is like that as well. I have learned to smile, I have learned to cry. I have learned to smile while I cry, and cry while I smile. I have spent long nights alone only to learn I was never really alone. I have questioned God only to realize that my pithy questions did not render Him any less God. Just as in our two years "On the Virge", I have summited mountains, viewed vistas, and made new friends. I have found myself disappointed by those who should have done better, only to discover unspeakable beauty in unlikely places. I have watched the ocean turn over the sand and recreate a beautiful beach while the sun shared her first light, and I have stared into a night sky that revealed a million stars I had once only imagined were there.

And this Journey, just like the Journey of our life, will now all too soon be complete.

Please keep in mind that the words in this book were written as they happened. The question I have posed repeatedly has been: "Will there be a YEAR 3?" I have even shared the anxiety that I have felt not knowing where my life would be going at the end of these two years. I want a fire to light the night and a cloud to show the way during the day. I'm not even opposed to some manna along the way. I have had the privilege of enjoying that level of confidence for these first two years. I would like to have the same confidence for a YEAR 3 and beyond.

So what is the answer to the question: Will there be a YEAR 3"? Here it is. I have come to believe that this was the wrong question all along. God has taught me an invaluable lesson over the last few months of the Journey, one that I have been hesitant to learn.

My Father-in-Law is a unique individual. As you recall, in their mid seventies, he and my Mother-in_law sold their family home and hit the road in their RV to volunteer building Churches and Youth camps all across the country. They have been gone months at a time. On one occasion I spent a few days with these "old" men and women, and was reminded again that age is merely a frame of mind. These people know how to work, how to pray and how to love each other. I made casual reference in an earlier chapter that I had the opportunity to help my Father-in-Law with a small project. His "small" project? He was building a house with his own hands. He began this project at age 78. Working beside him is a joy, and then again it's not. He can still work me into the ground.

My Father-in-Law has a few thousand sayings, most of which require a copy of the "East Texas Dictionary" to decipher. One of those that he recently shared with me at a low place in my life was this: "Getting old is not for the weak. If it was, everyone would do it".

I believe him to be correct. I cannot speak for everyone, only for me. Getting older has not been easy. Standing by the side of the highway looking down the winding road ahead is exhilarating. Turning around and realizing the majority of the road lays behind you is sobering. I have enjoyed a wonderful life, and I am grateful today for every step of the

Journey. I have even learned to say, "Thank You for the rain".

It's just that easing past your prime is not pleasurable. I've enjoyed two wonderful careers, its just that time marches on right past me. I still believe I could put on my uniform, grab my badge and gun and jump into a patrol car right now. If someone decided to run from me on foot I believe I could still give chase. It's just that I also realize that I also might not be able to get out of bed the next morning, or the next or maybe even the next.

It is likewise difficult for me to accept that some might think my appearance or style of music has become dated and therefore of lesser value. I still believe I can use the skill set given by the Creator to get the job done. But then that "skinny jean" thing raises its ugly head again, or should I say raises its pant leg. Though I can still work my way around a piano, it is difficult to face the fact that I would not be the first choice in what has unfortunately become a highly secularized job market.

Don't misunderstand, planning for a YEAR 3 is good human logic. It is only smart to count the cost. It speaks of great logic. It's just that it's the middle word that sinks the boat: "human". It is *human* logic. The premise has been that if a, b and c are present, it is God's will to keep going into a YEAR 3. I believe now that God says to those who will listen, "forget a b and c, and just trust Me". I have watched God excel through a "Magnificent Disaster". I have survived yet another "March Madness" and commented about "How Funny" it seemed as I watched Him maneuver through my best plans to deliver on the spot blessings. I have witnessed Him break through defenses of iron and break stone cold hearts. Can I not yet trust Him... *completely*?

So if "Will there be a YEAR 3" is the wrong question, what is the correct one? The question should not be "can I trust God for the next year", but rather "am I willing to trust Him for the next moment?"

God has not spoken to me specifically about another year. I believe that the initial two year plan for this Journey was a gift He gave me because of my lack of faith. I have come to believe however, that His silence was the avenue to teach me yet another lesson. I am to trust Him moment by moment. For now, that is enough. I will do what I am doing until He points me in another direction whether that is one year, five years or five minutes.

A few years ago a national motel chain ran a lengthy ad campaign where the tag line was "We'll leave the light on for you". Leaving a light on has always been a sign of welcome. Well, the title of this final chapter has nothing to do with that. When I was a young man living out of state, I would often leave after Sunday evening services and drive long hours into the night simply because I just couldn't wait to get back home to see my parents. It was even more difficult to wait when the trip preceded a holiday. It was infinitely more difficult when my mom struggled with cancer through her last few months. However, the title didn't come from that either.

I enjoy reading, and one of my favorite topics is World War 2. I love reading the stories of the sacrifices of ordinary Americans, the "citizen soldiers". I love reading the stories of a unified home front. I especially enjoy reading about a time in our nation when there was such a clear delineation between good and evil. I close this work with one such story.

This is taken from the words of John Hornfischer as told in his work "The Fleet at Flood Tide". Hornfischer is a New York Times bestselling author and coincidentally, a fellow Texan. This is taken from his account of the epic naval air battle of 1944 that rendered the mighty Japanese fleet a non-threat for the remainder of the war. It is known as the Battle of the Philippine Sea, or more colloquially as the "Marianas Turkey Shoot".

Pilots extended their machines to the absolute limits of their range to take the fight to the enemy. Men who only a few years earlier were high school students now held in their hands the future of freedom as we have come to understand it. Risking their very lives, they turned towards their aircraft carriers late in the day. Long before satellites ringed the planet providing precise locations on a virtual map, they realized that if they didn't navigate a non descript ocean and fly directly to their carrier they would crash land, out of fuel and likely lost forever. It is also the story of a fleet Admiral, Mark Mitscher, and a courageous decision that he made making it possible for the men under his command to find their way home.

Hornfischer tells their story far better than I could ever hope to, so I will share his words.

"To improve the odds of the pilots finding their roosts, Mitscher had dispersed his three task groups more widely than usual. Expanding the task force's radius would make it an easier target for the fliers and allow carrier captains more sea room to maneuver during aircraft recovery. Winds were variable, and captains would struggle to hold course into the breeze. Tired pilots did not need their landing circles to intersect. Mitscher was about to do something else as well. He would enact an important rescue protocol—so important that he had not told his pilots about it in advance. The less they knew about it, the better he thought it would work.

Mitscher had started the fireworks show as soon as the first returning plane appeared on the radar. He passed the order over the TBS radio to his chief of staff, relaying it in a manner that would ring in the history of naval aviation: "Bald Eagle, this is Blue Jacket himself. Turn on the lights."

Not some of the lights. All of the lights. Running lights, truck lights, and glow lights tracing carrier flight decks. Star shells on parachutes fired by five-inch guns of the screen, flashlights brandished by crew on deck, and twenty-four-inch carbon arc searchlights pointed straight up to touch the stars.

Regardless, the plan's blinding reality hit the returning pilots as a shock, and then as a gift from heaven. That was why Mitscher had said nothing about it in advance. Picturing his pilots in extremis, low on fuel, exhausted, perhaps gravely wounded, he had wanted them to navigate home as best they could, using all the focus and precision of attention that comes from a belief that one's own calculations are a matter of life and death. "Their desperation to pull that trick would engage all their effort, conscious and otherwise, to bring them close," Arleigh Burke said. Then the light show would guide them the rest of the way

We stood open-mouthed on the deck for a moment at the sheer audacity of asking the Japs to come and get us, then a spontaneous cheer went up.... Let them come in if they dare! Japs or no Japs, the Navy was taking care of its own; our pilots were not expendable!"

from: Hornfischer, James D. *The Fleet at Flood Tide America at Total War in the Pacific 1944-1945.* Bantam Dell Pub Group, 2017.

My life, just like yours, has been a series of mountains and valleys, a combination of joy and heartache. There were days when the sun shone so brightly through the windshield that the air conditioner could barely keep up. There have been other nights so dark that I doubted that the same sun would ever rise again.

I do not know where these last miles of my life's Journey will lead, but I do know where this Journey of my lifetime will end. I also know someone will leave their light on for me. On the horizon is the glow from my mom's heavenly porch light. She stands and moves the delicate lace curtains away from the window as she wonders aloud to my dad, questioning how soon I will arrive so we can start the celebration. I can almost hear her ask: "When do you think Joey will get here"?

The light in Matt's room will be on as well. He'll be inside the door sitting on the edge of his bed strumming away on his guitar, worshipping and singing at the top of his lungs, "How Great is our God". Perhaps I can stand outside of his door once again and just listen for a little while, maybe for a long while. I won't chuckle. I promise.

God? He won't have to leave the light on. He *is* the light in that land. I'll have at least one more blessing to fall at His nail scarred feet and be grateful for. While I am no longer a young man with the fresh morning breeze blowing through my hair, I am also certainly not nearly as "old" as I was a few short years ago. Age *is* a frame of mind. There is yet some magic left to discover, a heretofore undiscovered adventure that lay just around the next curve. An experience that is inexplicably drawn out of my soul by the beauty of a sunset, the majesty of a never before seen mountain range or the constant rhythm of the tires crossing the expansion joints between the sections of concrete roadway.

Just like Admiral Mitscher, Jesus Christ went to the extreme to make certain that I could one day find my way back home. To the very God of the Ages, we were never expendable. He laid down His life to pay a debt of sin that I owed, but could never pay. He peered into the darkness of my lost soul and "turned on the lights". And he left them on.

I cannot predict, nor count on the future. I have learned however, from Matt's Journey, that I can choose to make every moment of today matter. I just pray I can finish the last miles of this Journey of my lifetime in such a way that the first words I hear will be "well done".

THE GREATER JOURNEY...

My friend, do you have the assurance that your life's Journey will end in the presence of Jesus Christ? Do you know for certain that his blood has covered your sins? Have you trusted in Him for the ultimate salvation of your soul?

> *First, you must acknowledge that you have sinned, and that you have failed God, and that there is a punishment for that sin. See Romans 3:23 and 6:23a*

> *Second, you must realize that Jesus Christ made the way for you to find forgiveness for your sins by giving His life on the cross for you. He took that punishment for you. See Romans 6:23b and John 3:16*

> *Third, you must receive Him into your heart, the very core of your foundation and ask for his forgiveness. See Romans 10:9, 10*

If you have just trusted Christ and you asked Him to save you, you too can count on this: No matter how dark the night, He will always leave the light on for you to get home.

Why not tell someone about your decision? Someone you trust that attends a Bible believing church, or you can contact me. Go to our website at www.joeknight.us and send me an email.

Joe KNIGHT served as a Worship Leader and Police Officer for more than thirty-five years. He currently travels the country with his wife Shaunda sharing their incredible message of hope contained in this book in the *"The Journey of a Lifetime* Live Worship Event". He also shares through his music and real life experiences from his second book STORIES FROM THE ROAD, *Lessons From Life... and Death.*

Starting it all was the original story of the loss of their son Matt in his third year of Bible College in THE GREATER JOURNEY Live Worship Event. This is the subject of Joe's first book, TEARS IN A BOTTLE... *Lessons From A Broken Heart.* This work is available on your favorite book retailer's website or from www.joeknight.us.

To have Joe and Shaunda at your church or event, please visit the website or email Joe for details.

KNIGHTsong Ministries
A 501(c)(3) tax exempt Ministry Association
www.joeknight.us
knightjoew@gmail.com